THEY JUST DON'T GET IT

Communication and the Work of an Intermediary with Vulnerable People in the Justice System

by

Paula Backen

Dedication

This book is dedicated to June and Henry Backen who always said I could do anything if I wanted to, and continue to encourage me every day.

Acknowledgements

When I meet a client who is either my age, or the age of my two daughters, I reflect on the frequent lack of advantage in their lives compared with our own. *"There but for the grace of God go I"*. I say this not as a religious person, but as a true believer in equality of opportunity. This belief helps me to work with both witnesses and defendants in the legal system, the latter often victims themselves. Although of course, every name and story has been anonymised, I thank all those who have shared some of their lives with me, and made this book possible. Some may recognise parts of their story, but much has been mixed to achieve that anonymity.

Thanks to my Intermediary colleagues for long hours chatting about the crazy world we inhabit, and to all those friends whose interest has gently nudged me to complete this project. Thanks also to Andrew Linden for his creative design of my book cover.

Thank you, Delia, for generously hosting me in peaceful West Cork, to get the best part of this project off the ground (or down on paper). And last but no means least, thanks to Joyce for her never-ending graceful encouragement and enthusiasm.

"I don't need to go to court, I am in prison already!"

Abbie went to the local magistrates' court at least a couple of times a year. With nearly 30 appearances for various criminal offences, she could almost call it her second home. That would be just fine if she had a first home. Abbie sometimes slept in a tent in a friend's garden but most of the time she was homeless, sometimes sleeping in a nearby church graveyard. She was well known to the local police and usually recognised by court security staff when she turned up. But she did not always turn up; on one occasion when the court warned her to attend she was missing for 10 days, only to be found in a hospital bed having broken several bones. She had jumped off a bridge. Abbie had been diagnosed with Learning Difficulties but had rarely attended school and, by the age of 23 when I met her, she had learned important survival strategies. It was hard to determine her specific needs and she had no family or agency support. The first time we met, she was on remand. She told me that prison was great, as there were lots of women to take care of her and she was having fun tricking the prison guards, playing dead when they entered her prison cell. She had been given some almost new trainers by another inmate and had made plenty of friends. When I mentioned meeting her in court the following week, she replied that she was already in prison, so why would she need to go to court?

When Abbie attended court, she did not understand the vocabulary, could not read the oath or any case papers, and did not understand the words of the arraignment (or charge sheet). She did not know the difference between remand and sentence. Sometimes she asked me what she was in trouble for this time. She lived in the present, enjoyed the odd joke with a probation officer or shared a cigarette with a mate outside the courtroom. Until one day she achieved something she really wanted - she succeeded in ending her own life.

As with many defendants I have worked with, she was both a victim and a criminal. Along with many others who will appear in this book, she motivates me every day to work as an Intermediary. She did not engage with mental health or social services, but a just society looks out for its vulnerable people and when she reached the criminal justice system, her needs were not considered.

There were numerous assumptions which blocked her ability to participate actively: the assumption that she knew the charges against her, that she understood the roles of the people in the courtroom, that she appreciated her right to give evidence or change her plea.

Entitlement to a fair trial includes being able to understand and be involved in what is happening. The court decides who is considered 'fit to plead', to 'have capacity' or just "*looks like he is managing fine*". But being able to participate effectively is a real challenge for every vulnerable person.

The Registered Intermediary Scheme started as a pilot to address the needs of witnesses who were deemed vulnerable in the criminal courts, following the Youth Justice and Criminal Evidence Act 1999.[1] The service initially also included defendants but this was withdrawn in 2011. [I will address the definition of vulnerable later in the book.]

Although Registered Intermediary is a defined profession by the Ministry of Justice (MoJ), and seen as different from other (non-registered) Intermediaries who are not regulated or centrally trained, for simplicity, I will refer to all my work as that of an Intermediary throughout this book. At a personal level, wherever I work in the legal system, I am an Intermediary; whether the client is a prosecution witness, a defendant, a defence witness, a suspect or a complainant in a family hearing. The only difference for me is that the MoJ has not yet expanded its registration scheme.

The MoJ recruited experienced professionals with a background in special needs and communication and offered a short training course to prepare them for the role of Intermediary. As a neutral professional with a duty to the court, the Intermediary assesses and advises others on strategies and adjustments that will enhance communication, both in understanding and expressing ideas and thoughts when giving evidence to the police and for cross-

---

[1] This book describes the justice system in England and Wales only. Scotland operates without intermediaries. Northern Ireland has adopted a similar system for witnesses and - unlike England and Wales -extends the service to defendants giving evidence at trial.

examination in the courtroom. The Intermediary is a specialist in communication, a non-legal advisor in the legal system.

In the past decade, the Intermediary service has grown substantially and many more practitioners have been recruited by the MoJ, but the service continues to limit the scope of the scheme to witnesses in criminal cases.

In 2009, the Coroners and Justice Act (section 104) specified that vulnerable defendants should have access to a similar Intermediary service when they were giving evidence. At the time of writing this book in 2017, the MoJ has not yet provided this equity of service.

It was a chance remark from a close friend that introduced me to Naomi Mason. As one of the first Registered Intermediaries, n 2011 Naomi decided to respond to the growing demand for a similar service for defendants. She invited me to attend an independently-run training course and then join a new private agency, Communicourt. At the time of writing, Communicourt, and another agency Triangle, continue to provide most of the Intermediaries for defendants.

Since 2011 I have worked with hundreds of defendants, and after completing the MoJ Registered Intermediary training, have worked with a similar number of witnesses, in over sixty criminal and family courts across England and Wales.

This book is the result of my anger. This may sound strange until I explain. My other current work is as a consultant in anger management. I view anger as a valid and useful emotion which can be the motivation for real change. Rage (the aggressive expression of anger) is a problem; but anger is a natural feeling as part of the human condition and can be a motivation toward good.

I am angry when I get to court and see how the conventions of the justice system do not allow a vulnerable person to participate actively. I am annoyed when I hear that a man with an IQ of 51 is standing trial for murder, but there is not an available Intermediary to assist him at court; I am frustrated when I hear a court say that a suspect was read the caution in the police station, when I know this vulnerable person could not possibly have understood the complex language of the caution; I am angry when I am told by a judge that an Intermediary will sway the jury in a negative way, and it is preferable that I am hidden from view; I am irritated when ...

I could go on, but I would rather use the pages of this book to provide some insight into the realities of the role of an Intermediary in the current justice system and how vulnerable people need to be treated fairly.

Related professions such as lawyers, judges and researchers have talked and written about our work (often in praiseworthy terms) but Intermediaries have mostly only expressed their experiences through conferences and research work. In 2015 the first book about the Intermediary scheme was written by Joyce Plotnikoff and Richard Woolfson (1)[2], and led the way in describing the

---

[2] Please refer to the end of this book for 'Notes' for all numbered references.

details of the implementation and effects of the Intermediary in the justice system. Their book is intensely thorough and comprehensive. If my book succeeds in awakening your interest in this topic, then their book will fill in all the details and facts I have left out.

I hope this book will be of interest to anyone who cares about the way our legal system works and wants to gain a better understanding of the challenges of communicating with vulnerable people. I hope it will encourage my colleagues to write, and fill the gaps I have surely missed. I feel very privileged to have fallen into this profession and most grateful to Naomi for taking that first leap of faith with the defendant service.

I have not attempted to write a 'how to' manual. This book draws on my experiences, and discussions with colleagues and does not purport to cover the full range of work of an Intermediary. For example, I do not work with children under 12 years, which is a significant proportion of the witness referrals made to the Registered Intermediary service. I do not work with non-verbal or deaf clients either. My caseload is predominantly teenagers and adults. However, the issues and the experiences I draw upon can be generalised in many ways.

I have contemplated who is my target audience for far too long. In the end, I decided to leave it to you, the reader, to decide if this interests you. In some respects, this urge to decide who I am writing for suggests I know what you want. And in many ways, that is what we do with our clients in the legal system – we think we know what they want...and need. The most effective communication is a two-way process and I look forward to hearing your thoughts.

If you are a legal professional, an Intermediary, a law student or have served on a jury, you will be familiar with the court system language. If, however, you only have TV and fictional descriptions to go by, many of which will either be from the USA or out of date, you might want to have a quick look at the brief glossary of terms I have added at the end of the book.

A brief comment on the style of writing in this book: I have spent the last six years adapting my, and others' communication, to be simple and clear. It can be a struggle at times to convert the jargon into simple vocabulary. I hope I write in a similar style. As a result, I have shied away from writing in academic publications. This book is a collection of reflections written in an informal style, and can be read as a series of blogs. The book has developed from short pieces I started to write on my numerous train journeys, partly as a cathartic exercise. This is not an apology but hopefully an explanation for what follows.

"That sounds like a good job – can I do it?"

I qualified as a Speech and Language Therapist in 1981 and then spent many years working in large acute hospitals. Much of my work involved providing therapy to adult patients who had suffered brain damage. Perhaps a road traffic accident, a Stroke or a progressive neurological condition had affected their ability to understand and communicate. Along with my specialist skills in assessment and therapy, I learned how to manage a large therapy service in one of the biggest hospitals in the country. I thought I understood how to work in the public sector. I experienced the constant demand of increasing caseloads and never-ending efficiency savings.

In the NHS, there was a collaboration between the various professional groups. A patient who suffered a Stroke could expect his care to be provided by a multi-disciplinary team of physiotherapists, nurses, doctors, occupational therapists and healthcare assistants. For example, if a patient was struggling with eating after a Stroke, the physio might assist in adapting his sitting posture, the occupational therapist might provide suitable cutlery and help with hand-eye coordination, the dietician might advise on nutrition, whilst the speech & language therapist might be involved in deciding which food consistencies were easiest for him to swallow and how he could indicate his choice on a pictorial menu when he was unable to speak. There were overlaps in our professional knowledge and we certainly learned from each other, sometimes physically working alongside each other and at other times in individual treatment sessions. There was indeed a long-standing hierarchy, with doctors taking overall responsibility for an in-patient. I do recall doctors concluding that patients were more able than the therapist advised, often through lack of specialist knowledge of communication. For example, if the patient recovering from a Stroke responded 'yes' or 'no' to questions when the doctor was nodding or shaking his head suggestively, the doctor would conclude that the patient must surely be understanding everything; even though a speech therapy assessment had found him to have very limited understanding of words without a non-verbal cue.

There were plenty of rules and regulations, traditions and practices, lots of treatment changes resulting from research findings, new medications and procedures for the evolving needs of the populations, as well as the perennial annual savings targets and financial constraints. The health service was and still is in a constant state of flux, and reorganisations came all too frequently. I learned that if I suggested a new approach as a pilot study, there were less resistance and only individuals at a local level to convince. For example, when our small rehabilitation unit wanted the staff who served lunch and discussed menus with patients to be different from the nursing staff who had just taken them to the toilet or discussed their catheter care in the rehabilitation unit, we called it a 'pilot' and identified staff by giving them a black and white 'waitress' uniform, and training them in the specific role.

Given this extensive experience, I did not realise how confusing it would be to transfer my skills to the legal sector. There were indeed many assumptions that needed un-assuming. The pilot study of Registered Intermediary Scheme in 2003 had already been implemented nationally by the time I trained in 2014. But Intermediaries were still the new kids on the block in a world full of traditional practices seemingly. I quickly observed a much slower and more resistant attitude to change. Although the MoJ training has been led by barristers, Intermediaries do not have legal training. The adversarial approach is an essential part of the criminal justice system and results in lots of 'argument'. This extends outside the courtroom to conferences and pre-trial meetings. This is an unfamiliar climate for ex-NHS professionals, and it conflicts with our neutral independent role, advising both sides. Interestingly, when I started to work in the family courts, where the adversarial approach is not so fundamental, I found it a little easier to collaborate and fit in.

Tradition seems particularly hard to break and new ways take a long time to reach every courtroom. In the health service, there is a well-publicised postcode lottery effect. A patient in one city may have access to a variety of treatments that are not be available in the next. In the court system, I realised very quickly that the 'postcode' alters from one courtroom to another within the same building, and one judge may see no reason to allow a practice that is commonplace in the neighbouring courtroom. Within one building within a fortnight, one judge agreed that I should speak directly to a barrister if I wanted to intervene, while the neighbouring judge said, *'not in my court'* and ask me to raise the palm of my hand and wait for him to give me permission to speak. The difference between these two methods has a major impact on the flow of communication during a tense cross-examination.

As an Intermediary, one day I find myself viewed as a symbol of change which is threatening centuries-old legal traditions and on the very next day I am a welcome conduit for adapting the environment to suit a vulnerable person. Much of the challenge of the work of an Intermediary seems currently to depend on which 'postcode' we find ourselves in.

The pilot witness Intermediary service in 2003 developed exponentially and most likely out of all proportion to that which was originally anticipated. The original founders, trainers Penny Cooper and David Wurtzel, and researchers Joyce Plotnikoff and Richard Woolfson often express their pride that the concept has been so well adopted. Currently the registered service for witnesses takes around 6000 referrals a year.

****

The name 'Intermediary' has its drawbacks. Essentially this profession aims to simplify and clarify communication so that accurate and coherent information is exchanged; but its title is rarely understood. Many people cannot pronounce the word and even more cannot spell it. In other English-speaking countries eg New Zealand they prefer to use the terms Communication Assistant or Communication Advisor and both are certainly more transparent in meaning. The issue of profession title is not new to me. Originally described as a 'speech therapist', the profession decided in a national vote in the 1990's to change to 'speech and language therapist'. I am not sure this was an enlightening decision. I worked in a Middle-Eastern country where our title 'communication specialist' meant that when the telephone engineers went on strike, our patients thought we would not be working either! Professions invariably argue about their given title, but as specialists in communication it seems even more relevant that we communicate what we do as clearly as possible.

In the courtroom, the name Intermediary is further confused as the first five letters coincide with interpreter and we are often assumed to be interpreting. Certainly, for the client who has very limited understanding, it may seem as if we are taking the complex Legalese and translating it into English. There is more to it of course; our clients may have mental health issues, traumatic brain injury affecting their insight, emotional regulation and verbal reasoning skills, and are often functionally illiterate.

In court, only legal advocates speak directly to the judge. This means that a solicitor who is supporting a barrister, or a police officer who had been involved in the case from the start, cannot address the court unless he is called as witness. Intermediaries are however permitted to address the court and intervene, although as mentioned above, it is dependent on each judge to approve the method of this intervention.

Other people who advise the court, such as expert witnesses are part of either prosecution or defence. For example, if a psychologist or psychiatrist is asked for a report, it is commissioned by one side or other and is part of a case. The information can be presented to the jury as evidence. An Intermediary is neutral and an officer of the court. If it works as intended, the Intermediary addresses and discusses her[3] findings and recommendations with the judge and legal advocates. The Intermediary does not appear in court as a witness, and so does not take an oath and is not cross-examined. Her report is not part of any evidence in a case. This is a novel situation for a courtroom and provides many challenges in implementing it. I have been inappropriately asked to take an oath, been cross-examined as if I am part of a prosecution / defence case, and on occasion there has been suggestions that the contents of my report be shared with the jury.

Whilst clearly the judge controls the whole trial process and has final responsibility for how questions are asked, an Intermediary can recommend how the environment may be changed to enhance communication, intervene during evidence to advise on questions, indicate the need for a break in open court and speak to a defendant whilst sitting beside him in the dock. In the dock, an Intermediary can simplify the proceedings, alert the defendant to events, and help to manage limited attention and concentration.

Aside from security dock officers and interpreters, Intermediaries are the only court professionals who spend any length of time in a

---

[3] For simplicity, I have used female pronouns for Intermediaries and male pronouns for vulnerable people, although of course both genders are represented.

court dock. This side of the work of an Intermediary with defendants can be intimidating; sitting behind a glass screen, beside a person who may well be convicted of serious crimes, with the door locked and the hard seats firmly screwed to the floor. These glass docks were introduced as recently as 2000 and there is no statutory requirement or judicial authority for their use in our courts (2). Defendants are legally considered innocent until proven otherwise by British law but that is not a feeling I recognise when I sit in the dock. Over time I have acclimatised to the experience but I try not to forget my first impression, as for the defendant this will often be their first experience and it can be daunting. The defendant can usually hear better and potentially engage more fully in his trial if he is sitting in the main body of the courtroom, or at least in an open non-glass-enclosed dock. Recently, in non-violent cases, I have been asking the judge to permit this alternative. The more comfortable chair, the availability of a desk to set out papers and visual aids and being present in the main part of the courtroom significantly changes the practical experience of a defendant.

A few years ago, I was called to assist Colin who was accused of joint enterprise murder. There were eight other defendants in the dock with him. As protocol requires, the defendants were seated in the order of the trial listing and I sat down beside Colin. Unfortunately, this meant I was sitting in the middle of the front row. Imagine the view from the jury area: a group of young lads with a middle-aged woman sitting centre stage. This was early on in my work as an Intermediary and a first for me. The trial was to last several weeks and this was just the first day. Sitting with a vulnerable defendant, I was feeling quite vulnerable myself. Colin was somewhat ambivalent about my assistance. He knew he needed help, but he did not want his vulnerability highlighted in front of his peers. There were two security officers in the dock. The usher came to the dock glass to pass a copy of a written transcript to me so I could help Colin follow it. One of the other defendants grabbed the papers and started to pass them around the group, keeping them away from Colin and me. When I reached for the papers, one of the defendants put his feet up on the back of my chair and whispered teasingly that he was not going to let me have them. I looked toward the dock officers for support but none was forthcoming. When the papers finally arrived in Colin's hands, he looked away from me and refused to respond to my comments.

I raised my hand to indicate to the judge that I required a break. The court was adjourned and I stepped outside the dock, feeling embarrassingly emotional. The usher approached me and I explained what had just happened. He took me out of the courtroom and one of the police officers showed me into a conference room. I was asked to explain what had happened and a written statement was taken. The statement was passed up to the judge and he ruled that the defendant had lost his right to the assistance of an Intermediary and I was told to go home. Interestingly Colin's defence barrister did not approach me or seek to become involved. I left feeling that I had failed in my job, knowing logically that I could not help a person who did not want to be helped. Of course, peer-pressure and groupthink can be a strong influence but I don't know if justice was done by putting those young men in a dock together. The space can be quite limited in smaller courtrooms, and the environment can have a significant effect on behaviour over long periods.

I am however certain that sitting in a dock is an experience that more barristers and judges need to have if they are to appreciate the struggle of many vulnerable defendants to participate in their trial. From some statistics collated on a population of 450 vulnerable defendants who were referred for an Intermediary service (3), almost half the cases involved a co-defendant. My advice these days is to request that, whatever the order of defendants, the vulnerable defendant is seated with the Intermediary at the end of the row.

Whilst on the topic of co-defendants, I attended another trial to assist Duncan, only to find that of his co-defendant Edward was probably as vulnerable as Duncan. Edward's barrister approached me as we waited for the trial to start and asked if I would be willing to also assist Edward. An interesting suggestion, but clearly not practical. Without assessing Edward, I could not know what his communication needs or how best to help him. How would I in practical terms be in both men's conferences with their barristers at the same time? Perhaps the advocate had confused me with an interpreter, or perhaps it was just wishful thinking at this late stage when he realised that Edward had his own special needs. When Edward went into the witness box, he struggled to cope with questions and raised his T-shirt to cover his embarrassed face, revealing his bare chest. The judge reprimanded him and Edward struggled to continue with answering questions. I was in the dock beside Colin while this took place and was dismayed to think that Edward could have benefitted from an Intermediary if his solicitor had recognised his needs ahead of the trial.

The likelihood of the solicitor doing so is dependent on their experience. If the solicitor's firm has engaged Intermediaries in the past, then it is more likely to be alert to the needs of the next vulnerable client. I receive at least one referral per month from two offices of a one firm, but none from the other three offices of the same firm, even though they provide a service to a similar client population in their geographical area. This may just be the process of spreading the word, as there is no national coordinated approach for defendants. For witnesses, referrals depend on Crown Prosecution Service (CPS) or police forces recognising vulnerability and referral patterns are certainly not even across the country. Post code lottery remains an issue in this regard also.

****

Ferne was just 16 years old when she was referred to me as a vulnerable witness. Following an alleged traumatic sexual incident when she was 14 years old, she had not allowed anyone, including her mother and sister, to enter her personal physical space. Her sole comfort was a small dog who sat on her lap, followed her around the house and slept in her bed. I successfully requested that the court allow this small dog during cross-examination to enable Ferne to give her 'best evidence'.

Achieving 'best evidence' 'is a term used to indicate the objective of the justice system to encourage optimum conditions for hearing what actually happened. Evidence is core to our justice system that relies so heavily upon an oral tradition. A recent publication (4) referred to enabling a process which allows '*those giving evidence to do so to the best of their ability and in the most accurate and comprehensive way possible*'. Ferne's dog was her enabler and she could answer questions with increased confidence.

Gobi was charged with a public disorder offence. When I first met him, he was unsure if he was *"in trouble"* or if he was the victim of a crime. His solicitor was not present when I assessed him, and his father did not speak sufficient English to clarify the situation. I contacted his solicitor after the assessment and we agreed that it would be useful if I could assist her to take instructions from Gobi. I helped in simplifying and structuring the solicitor's questions and then with the use of visual aids, helped Gobi to sequence the events as he recalled them. His solicitor later reflected that the involvement of an Intermediary was vital to her success in preparing the case.

This is how Gobi explained his story: Gobi was generally accompanied everywhere by a family member. Unusually he had been out alone one day when he was befriended by an older man and spent three days wandering across a big city lending him money whenever he was asked. On the third day, the older man promised to withdraw cash from an ATM to repay Gobi. However, when the machine declined his card, a fight broke out and some passers-by called the police. They were both charged with a public order offence. Gobi was very frightened by the whole event. With Learning Difficulties and highly dependent on his family for all his daily needs, his communication skills were not sufficient to participate effectively in court. He expressed his fear about being expected to sit beside this co-defendant in the dock, or even to be seen by him in the court building. In some respects, he was more of a victim than a defendant. Following my recommendations, the magistrates agreed to Gobi attending court via a live (or virtual) link for the entire trial. I was permitted to sit beside him and explain the proceedings and when he was called to give evidence, it was from the link room. Gobi had very limited communication skills and was very fearful, but these special measures certainly allowed him to participate in his trial.

There are many special measures now permitted in the courtroom which are so frequently implemented as to be common-place (5). For example, alleged victims of sexual offences may give video-recorded evidence in advance and then are cross-examined via a live link thereby avoiding the intimidating courtroom or seeing the defendant. A crown court can be asked to remove wigs and gowns if this helps to reduce a witness's anxiety. Screens can be placed around the witness box to protect the witness from being viewed by the defendant or the public gallery. More recently, following a successful pilot scheme, the cross-examination of a witness can take place in advance of the trial and is then played as a video-recording, thus avoiding the need for the witness to attend the court at the time of the trial. This scheme (section 28 of the Youth Justice and Criminal Evidence Act 1999 is the last special measure to be implemented) is now being rolled out nationally.

As each new special measure is experienced by a court and judge, it becomes a part of their repertoire, but in an idiosyncratic manner. For example, in some areas the CPS may expect all vulnerable witnesses to want the use of screens around the witness box or all of them to give evidence from a live link room. The former shields the witness from being seen by and seeing the defendant. The latter avoids the need for a witness to enter the daunting courtroom and the need to speak in front of a lot of people. A live link room, usually in the same court building, allows the witness to sit with the Intermediary and speak via a large TV monitor to the questioner. However, the acceptance of these measures varies enormously between courts. Sometimes the repertoire is narrowed to what has been 'successful' for a particular barrister. I have been told by police officers in some locations that the CPS do not want 'their' witnesses in a link room as the jury does not see the full impact of the witness's demeanour. On other occasions, I have heard the reverse opinion; if the witness comes into court, the CPS is worried the witness will be unpredictable and so prefers a link room. A rule for all vulnerable witnesses does not recognise the individual needs of each and every witness. An Intermediary will look at the best environment for the individual witness and advise the court accordingly.

In some instances, the resistance is based on practicalities. Link rooms, where a monitor is linked to the courtroom (similar to a Skype or FaceTime session), are relatively new to the courts. When allocating a suitable room, the choices have been limited in court buildings built at the beginning of the last century. I have been in link rooms no bigger than a stationary cupboard and both claustrophobic and unsuitable. Witnesses may need to be in these rooms for multiple hour-long sessions, accompanied by an usher and an Intermediary crammed into the space. Unsurprisingly, I have encountered several witnesses who chose to go into court rather than sit in such a room. Other courts, more recently built have spacious and comfortable link rooms.

One of the issues with link rooms is that the defendant and public can view the witness via a large TV monitor. By opting for the link room, the witness may be unwittingly giving the defendant a clear view of her. Often the witness does not want to be viewed by a defendant, as she may be frightened or intimidated, or perhaps worried about future recriminations.

I met Zelda initially at her home, where she exhibited some intense panic attacks and disassociations. She was clearly very afraid of her alleged perpetrator. I attended a crown court hearing where I advised the judge that Zelda would benefit from being in a link room, as she was too anxious to speak in a large room with many staring faces. She also wanted to be reassured that the defendant could not see her face. The judge did not accept this and told me to go back to Zelda and offer her a choice between the two measures – either come into court behind screen or use the link room. I remonstrated, insisting that this was an accepted special measure and my recommendation had been accepted in other courts. Her Honour's reply was '*not in my court*'.

A few months later, I worked with Beatrice for whom I had similarly recommended this special measure. As I entered the court, I realised that the above-mentioned judge was presiding in this case. She indicated that she also recognised me, acknowledged that she had read my report and anticipated I would be asking for the combination of live link and screening the defendant. This time she explained that she had considered the matter and had found a way in this courtroom to implement my recommendation. She asked for the large TV monitors to be turned off, and small monitors placed in front of the jury. In this way, everyone had access to a monitor except the defendant, but as the judge explained, she felt it was not incriminating him by explicitly excluding him.

This judge had accepted a recommendation she had previously rejected. I came away from that court feeling very hopeful for the future. It was possible to change minds. I just needed to be more patient.

Working within the environment of so many courts, with constantly changing personnel, clearly has its disadvantages.

****

So, is this a job that I would recommend to my friends? It is very isolating; there is no consistent team to belong to, no regular office or place of work. Every case usually involves meeting a new set of people – police officers, lawyers, support services and court staff. If the Intermediary sticks to a small geographical patch, then some relationships can develop at a local level. I chose to take work across England and Wales, and as such rarely meet anyone for more than one case. When I do, it is a great relief as a rapport has already been established.

I miss the easy-going nature of working with familiar people, with whom you have established working practices and developed ideas in a supportive environment from my previous career in the NHS. Conversely, perhaps repeatedly working with the same people can result in less willingness to change and more complacency about the work. I often think that with every new case, it is similar to the first day in a new job.

In the role of Intermediary, I certainly need to establish credibility very rapidly. How this is done is clearly an art not a science and is very difficult to teach. One of my memories of the selection process for becoming a Registered Intermediary, was being asked to explain how my credibility will be established in a new environment, as this was an important person specification for the role. With every case, there is the 'Groundhog Day' feeling as I seek the trust and acceptance of the lawyers, the police and the court staff. Sometimes I am affected by whether an Intermediary has preceded me – my first question is usually "*Have you ever worked with an Intermediary before?*" Mostly this is met with positive recounts, but they may just be being polite (6) – all professions have their full range of competencies and of course there could be simply a clash or clicking of personalities. Unlike many other professions, Registered Intermediaries have very little peer review and no management structure for supervision.

A sample week from my diary revealed a hugely varied diet. Monday, I planned to meet Jo, an alleged victim of domestic violence. This was to be my second meeting with her and she had agreed to come on a pre-trial court visit, to become more familiar with the building and what would be expected of her on the day of the trial. She had been very reticent to become involved with a trial, having previously been a defendant in a magistrates' court for minor offences, and in this case, was being harassed by the defendant's family to withdraw her complaints. On my way to meet her, I took a call from her social worker who explained that Jo had texted to say she was too poorly to leave her house and subsequently had refused to answer her phone. My journey was in vain and I returned home.

Tuesday, I set off to see an elderly suspect. The police had previously met with an alleged victim of historic abuse and needed to interview 90-year old Herbert as the identified alleged perpetrator. The police officer had quickly become concerned about his level of communication. Herbert had suffered a Stroke several years prior to this meeting, and although he lived alone, he struggled to communicate his needs to the carers who visited him twice daily. I carried out a preliminary assessment of his verbal comprehension. His sons and the police officers watched and became increasingly surprised at how little he could understand when context, non-verbal cues and gestures were removed. I asked him to point to his son. He looked me in the eye and said "*Yes*". For the following three questions, which required pointing or giving me an object, he responded only "*Yes*". My assessment revealed that he could not be reliably interviewed, and within an hour, the officer had decided she would be recommending that the case be closed. I had saved the police time and the justice system money in what would most likely have been a protracted investigation lasting up to two years, and raising unrealistic expectations for the alleged victim.

Onto Wednesday, and time to see Isaac, a young man diagnosed with Autistic Spectrum Disorder and Learning Difficulties who attended the solicitor's office with his father. Isaac had two criminal cases pending. From my assessment, I concluded that he would clearly benefit from an Intermediary and I prepared a report for the court.

The family jurisdiction case on Thursday involved Janice, a young mother facing a court hearing to decide whether to permanently remove her one-year-old daughter from her care. Janice could not read, had very limited experience of life, numerous exaggerated fears of the world and told me she had not understood the '*posh words*' spoken in court. Janice had been a victim of abuse as a small child and described her experience of using a live link to the court when she had given evidence. She asked if I could arrange this again for her.

In just one week, I had worked in criminal and family law cases, with a witness, a defendant, a respondent and a suspect. Common to each case was the core objective to assess and advise how to maximise communication in the legal system.

Sometimes the limited nature of my involvement with a client can feel unsatisfying. It took several months and many meetings for Kim to tell the details of sexual abuse to an interviewing officer. The evidence was related to events that had taken place over several years and involved many suspects. The final bundle submitted to court was made up of ten DVDs. There was a long-term relationship between the interviewing officer, supporting officers, a social worker and this witness. The referral for my involvement as an Intermediary did not come until the trial date was planned, nearly two years after the first DVD had been recorded. Kim showed some justifiable resistance to establishing rapport with me, as I was yet another professional involved in her case. Indeed, this can be a 'big ask' for traumatised people, when trust does not come easy after their experiences. My role was highly circumscribed – I was, as usual, required to end my involvement as soon as Kim completed her evidence and her day in court – whilst the officers could arrange a gradual reduction in their relationship which had developed over years.

Sometimes the recommendations I have made have either not been accepted or have not been practical. A local woman was reported to be taking advantage of several vulnerable people in her area. She befriended them and once she was invited into their homes she allegedly stole a variety of items. Two of these alleged victims, Jack and John, were referred to me for assessment. Both had spent some time in psychiatric asylums as young adults, but since the 'Care in the Community' policies of recent decades they had both moved to independent-living flats with support packages from community mental health teams. After my assessment, I reported to the court that they would both benefit from a range of adaptations at court. In view of their heightened anxiety which would seriously limit their ability to respond to cross-examination, I suggested that they should only be warned to arrive at court an hour or so before they were required. The standard witness arrangement is a warning to attend court for every day of the listed trial from 9.00 in the morning. Jack told me he had received a letter that he must be in court for five days. Their expected time in the witness box was unlikely to be more than an hour in total. I spoke with the Officer in the Case (OiC), and she tried to convince the CPS to delay their arrival time. In effect, in most trials in a crown court, by the time there has been some legal arguments, the jury has been empanelled, an opening speech has been made by the prosecutor, and the recording of their evidence has been played, it is lunchtime. This could delay a witness being called into court for up to 5 hours, time spent in a small enclosed area where a witness service volunteer needs to escort them down many corridors to an appropriate exit for any cigarette break. However, the CPS were insistent that both Jack and John arrive at 9.00am.

I have experienced extended waiting periods in a court, and it has left me undecided about the benefits of limiting the wait for some highly anxious witnesses. Bill and Bob, both witnesses, needed my assistance with cross-examination. Both had been diagnosed with Autistic Spectrum Disorder and were prescribed medication for high anxiety states. They were both warned to attend court on a Monday morning. In his extremely anxious state, Bob had left the country on a flight to Europe the previous Friday. Only with repeated coaxing by his friend Bill via texts and phone calls, Bob eventually returned on Thursday.

Each morning, Bill came to the court witness service area. On Monday, Bill arrived visibly uneasy and almost unable to speak. Various strategies we had practised to reduce anxiety were to no avail. When it was clear Bob was not coming, the court adjourned and we all went home. Returning each subsequent day, I noticed Bill becoming progressively less anxious. By Thursday when Bob finally arrived, I reported to the judge that both witnesses were ready to proceed, and Bill had relaxed considerably, becoming quite blasé about the court environment. This led me to think that perhaps long waiting periods could, in some cases, be beneficial.

In the earlier case of Jack and John, we all arrived at court around 9.30 and found two other witnesses also involved in the case who had been warned for that morning. All the witnesses were taken to a separate waiting area run by witness service. This was a small crown court, and in the general waiting area I noticed a woman arriving with what seemed to be her life possessions stuffed into carrier bags. She reorganised the packages and some of her clothing, and then went off to speak with a barrister. On her return, she announced loudly to the entire public waiting room that she was *"going guilty"*. This was in fact the defendant in Jack and John's case. Soon afterward we were told that there would be a guilty plea and all the witnesses could go home. The prosecuting barrister thanked Jack and John for attending and emphasised the importance of their presence at court, as this had affected the defendant's decision to plead.

There is clearly a balance to be found between keeping vulnerable people waiting unnecessarily and ensuring the defendant knows the complainants have arrived. Jack was distressed and confused by the change of plan. It took repeated explanations to convince him that there was no need to return to court on subsequent days and that he could think ahead now without any of the stress of the case.

A guilty plea on the morning of the trial can be a relief for some witnesses. For others, it robs them of an opportunity to tell the court what had happened. This need is often lost in the concern to protect a vulnerable witness. It is indeed so difficult to predict the preferences of a witness. I recall a situation in court where the judge was determined that the defence barrister would not be allowed to 'put his case' to Suzannah, the alleged victim. When we left court Suzannah complained that the barrister had not called her a liar and she had not had a chance to say passionately that '*he did it!*'

****

Significant resources are employed to bring a case to the point of trial. In my experience, many crown court cases take around two years to get to trial and magistrates' court cases can take well over a year. The ever-increasing workload of the police investigating and supporting the witnesses, the costs of involving of Intermediaries in the preparation for trial and the strain on vulnerable people and their families cannot be minimised. All the pre-trial work is essential and without it there would not be justice for the proven crimes. Cases fall before trial for many different reasons and the Intermediary may not be a party to these decisions. The CPS decide if it is in the public interest to proceed and the defendant can potentially choose at any time to change his plea. In some instances, the witness needs assistance from the Intermediary to understand a subtle change of plea.

Before any of this is possible, the alleged victim must be willing to tell the police what happened. One morning I set out to see Lianne who I had already assisted in two other police interviews over a period of three years. This was the third time Lianne had reported an incident to the police and the officer wanted my involvement to maintain continuity. I remembered that the two previous cases had not progressed to any charges or trial. The train journey took three hours and as I was arriving in the area, I contacted the officer to let her know my train was running to time. She informed me that Lianne was declining to participate in the planned meeting, and after one call and a couple of texts, was now ignoring further communication. I suggested that the officer explain that I had travelled a long way and hadn't seen her for over a year and would like to meet up at least for a coffee and a chat. An hour and a half later, despite the officer visiting her at home, the meeting was cancelled. I am acutely aware that police funds are stretched and appreciate the frustration that results from having to pay for a service that was not used. I also repeatedly feel frustrated that other witnesses and defendants are being delayed in receiving an Intermediary service as our diaries fill up so quickly. However, we are dealing with people: people are complex and vulnerable people are even more complex.

I am constantly reminded of the unpredictability of this work. Here is a random week when I had recorded the difference between my anticipated plans and actual experience.

Sunday evening, I was just thinking how unusually predictable my week ahead was going to be. I had been booked for three different courts over four days: two crown courts with witnesses I had seen recently, with counsel and judges I had agreed ground rules and commented on questions in advance, along with a magistrates' court with a defendant where I had already agreed some ground rules. What could change?

By Friday, I had only worked for two hours in total and none of the three trials had needed me. One trial was postponed for several months; in another, the case had been closed as prosecution had decided there was insufficient evidence; and the third case was overrunning into the following week, when I was already booked up and therefore could not assist.

For the vulnerable person, this unpredictability makes a traumatic event more so. Trust is such an issue for traumatised individuals; how can you possibly trust a system that cannot promise what will happen and when? I met Tina for an assessment and she told me her trial had been booked for July. As no Intermediary was available at that time, the trial was then relisted for April of the following year. On the first day of the trial, we found out that instead of the trial being 'fixed' (meaning it had an allocated judge and courtroom), as is usually done for trials with Intermediaries, we were a 'floater'. This meant we were dependent on another case finishing earlier than expected or not being able to start. Tina arrived at court at 8.30am, highly anxious after a difficult journey from home. By 11am it was clear there would be some delay. At 2.15pm we were told to move to another court building where a courtroom and judge had been identified to take the case. Tina and her family were unsure if they had sufficient cash to make the train and taxi journey. After an hour in that court, the judge indicated he would not be available for the final day of the four-day trial, so the following morning we moved to the third court building in the county, with a new judge. So much uncertainty for a highly anxious vulnerable person.

Clearly being an Intermediary is not a job for anyone who likes routine, consistency or predictability.

"*This country is broke, we don't have time for a Ground Rules Hearing*"

A Ground Rules Hearing (GRH) is a new type of hearing introduced to the court proceedings, initiated as far as I understand, as a method to discuss with and forewarn the lawyers of issues or 'ground rules' which might otherwise trigger the judge's intervention at trial. (The term was first used by California judges specifying what would and would not be allowed in the questioning of children.) The hearing helps ensure that the court considers the findings of the Intermediary report and other special measures prior to the trial commencing, and that there is an opportunity for the Intermediary to address the court. I have been asked to speak from the witness stand, in other courts I sit behind the advocates. If the latter, I make a point of sitting midway between prosecution and defence to reinforce my neutral position.

The GRH ensures the Intermediary has authorisation for her involvement in the trial, for example how to intervene, where she will sit, how she will be explained to the jury, the way questions will be phrased and the timings of breaks. Other matters are addressed, such as the need for visual aids to ensure the witness has understood the question, the time of day which best facilitates alertness in a person in poor physical or mental health, or the need for additional microphones to ensure the court can hear a very quietly spoken witness. The use of the live link room, the screening of the witness, the use of a remote link away from the courtroom and perhaps, if appropriate, the arrangement for the judge and advocates to meet the witness before she comes into court. For the defendant, there may be issues such as how long he can concentrate on listening to evidence, whether he may be permitted to use stress relieving activities such as tangle toys, or whether the Intermediary can assist with note-taking in the dock.

A few years ago, I asked the defence barrister if she could request a GRH when we started the trial. The defendant was already in the dock, so I went to sit beside him. The judge addressed me directly saying *"Are you an experienced Intermediary?"* to which I quickly stood up and replied, *"I am, Your Honour"*. He retorted *"Well then, just get on with it. This country is broke and we don't have time for such matters"*.

Over time, I have noticed an increasing acceptance of the need for a GRH, but despite it being a procedural requirement, it is not happening in every courtroom where there is an Intermediary involved and some of the hearings are perfunctory. Judges often suggest that, as everyone has read my report, we can just proceed. My reports now include a 'Suggested agenda for GRH' on the last page, in the hope this will highlight the need for discussion and authorisation. And sometimes this works.

Some judges encourage me to take the court through the agenda, interjecting with queries, and checking that the barristers can comply with the recommendations. Others have fixed their opinions about the level of vulnerability before we start the hearing. Some barristers insist on asking me questions as if I am an expert witness and I am then 'cross-examined'. I can see how strange the role of the Intermediary can be for a legal system steeped in tradition and long-standing practice. The Intermediary is not a witness, not an advocate nor of course a judge, and she wants to communicate with the court in a very different manner. The Intermediary is not part of either defence or prosecution, but seeks to advise the court. On one occasion only, on the direction of the judge, the court adjourned to the judge's chambers for the GRH and we sat around a conference table. The environment reduced the formality and hierarchy of the courtroom. A clerk was present to take notes. This was one of the most productive GRHs I have experienced. A genuine sharing of ideas and an absence of adversarial controversy. I felt appreciated as part of a team of people seeking to find the best way to enable a vulnerable person to contribute to justice.

The communication dynamics were profoundly altered and I felt I was an equal part of a group discussing how best to manage this witness's experience of court.

GRHs were introduced to discuss the ground rules, which sounds obvious but needs to be said. I assisted in the development of a GRH checklist for advocates and judges, indicating the range of matters that would need addressing and the requirement of involving the Intermediary in the discussion in court.

In my reports, I always mention that I am willing to attend for any contested hearing, but have rarely been invited. However, I have now attended several GRHs where the time is being used for one side to contest the involvement of an Intermediary, a matter that should precede a GRH. A recent draft policy for West Midlands courts recommends that any contest regarding the involvement of the Intermediary should take place at the GRH. I am rarely invited to speak on these occasions, and the judge has dismissed the appointment of an intermediary without asking for any contribution from me. I do wonder at these times why I have been booked to attend. Decisions on the appointment of an Intermediary are sometimes made based on preconceived ideas of communication needs, or levels of vulnerability. Later I discuss the advice in an Intermediary report, but generally the court assumes that all Intermediaries recommend the need for an Intermediary in every report.

When ground rules have been agreed with a judge, I am able to do the rest of my work with some confidence. If during the proceedings I become concerned that a ground rule is not being adhered to, I can raise it with the judge. Without this agreement, I find myself apprehensive and unsure about how I will carry out my role. There have also been occasions when a second GRH was appropriate. During a lengthy trial, it has been useful to revisit a defendant's communicative needs just before he gives evidence.

****

Although the national roll-out of the Registered Intermediary service for witnesses was completed in 2008, the MoJ has yet to introduce a similar service for defendants. Introducing a new service, particularly for people who may have committed 'dreadful crimes', would not be a vote-winner. The costs of such a service have not been fully recognised. Or perhaps they have been recognised at Whitehall and that is the reason for the delay – I do not have that information.

We all know there is no spare cash in the justice system, as with all public services, and many more able writers have detailed the challenges to justice when money is tight. Even providing an Intermediary service to the few lucky defendants who win the postcode lottery, must be costing the justice system a lot of money. I hear you say, *"Can we afford it?"* I strongly believe that in many cases we can save money by involving an Intermediary in a vulnerable defendant's case.

Many vulnerable defendants with limited understanding and poor verbal reasoning believe that their best way to freedom is to deny a charge. They may plead not guilty despite overwhelming evidence to the contrary. In my experience, despite several meetings with their legal team, the defendant continues to believe their only option is to plead not guilty and go through with a trial. Once an Intermediary has assessed the defendant, the language can be adapted to ensure he fully understands the evidence and the options available in pleading guilty. I have met with many defendants, who once this is understood, change their plea. There is then no need for a trial and victims are spared the ordeal of attending court. This saves the courts considerable money and time. In addition, it may also save the prison budget, as a guilty plea may attract a shorter or lighter sentence.

Bobby was a suspect in a sexual assault case. When I assessed him, it was clear he had very limited comprehension of language and poor reasoning skills. He had been diagnosed with Learning Disabilities and lived on benefits with his step-sister. His barrister asked me to attend a pre-trial conference. He wanted to explain to Bobby that there had been some CCTV that showed him at the scene of the crime. Bobby continued to say he had been at his friend's party. I suggested to the barrister that we showed Bobby the CCTV evidence. Bobby had, like many other defendants with poor verbal reasoning, believed that if he continued to say, *"not guilty"*, the court would eventually believe him. However, once he understood the evidence fully he changed his plea. There was no need for a trial, the victim did not have to be cross-examined and Bobby was sentenced at a short hearing. This saved time and money.

In another case, Billy was accused of raping his friend. He pleaded 'not guilty'. At a pre-trial conference, the barrister told him there was *"DNA evidence"*. He repeated it several times and Billy continued to maintain his innocence. I thought about the likelihood of Billy understanding the meaning of the barrister's words. I simplified: *"They have found bits of your body in her knickers"*. With this, Billy finally understood and admitted his guilt. No trial and money saved.

Once the trial starts, costs may be reduced if the defendant fully understands the situation. For example, after the prosecution case has been heard in a trial, a judge may be asked by the defence advocate if he will offer a 'Goodyear'. In simple terms, this means that the judge can give a maximum sentencing indication if the defendant were to plead at this stage of the trial. Christopher had a verbal comprehension level of a 7-year-old and struggled to understand the complex conceptual nature of this offer. With my help, Christopher had an opportunity to appreciate the full situation and decided to take the lesser sentence option. This shortened the hearing and again saved the court budget.

In some cases, barristers find it very difficult to take instruction from a defendant with mental illness or poor concentration, verbosity and lack of insight. An Intermediary can speed up and simplify the process. As part of a family case, Sheila was referred for an Intermediary assessment. Sheila had already given her first child up for adoption and was being asked to agree to her second baby being adopted by Sheila's mother. Sheila was insightful about her own limitations as a carer, as she struggled with her own day-to-day needs and had made several suicide attempts. At the solicitor's office, I helped her explain in a logical order, using visual timelines, what she wanted for her baby. I simplified the written statement prepared by her solicitor, so Sheila could be sure she understood before signing. This moved the case on more rapidly and reduced the number of family court hearings.

I emphasise again here, that the Intermediary is neutral in all these discussions. My role is entirely focussed on maximising understanding and communication without prejudice. I think it will be clear throughout this book, that the crimes or circumstances of each case are not important to me. Whether a defendant is guilty, a witness is truly a victim, or if a mother can parent, is not my focus. I leave that to the lawyers, the expert witnesses and the final decision to the jury.

****

Recognising a vulnerability is also controversial in my experience. The legal system has a definition for 'vulnerable': either under 18 years old at the time of the hearing; suffering from a mental disorder within the meaning of the Mental Health Act 1983; otherwise has a significant impairment of intelligence and social functioning; or has a physical disability or physical disorder. If someone falls within these parameters their evidence is likely to be diminished in terms of completeness, coherence and accuracy.

Witnesses can be as young as two or three years old and there is an increasing acceptance of the value of such young people's evidence, with the appropriate assistance. The age of criminal responsibility is 10 years in England and Wales, even though the UN Commission on Rights of the Child has recommended raising the age to 15. I have met witnesses and defendants aged between 10 and 90. In recent years, I have noted an increase in very elderly suspects, perhaps because of increasing numbers of alleged victims of non-recent sexual crimes. When I worked for Communicourt, the largest Intermediary agency for defendants, I collected statistics on the caseload (3). Over 50% were aged between 13-25 and over 85% male.

I do not work with children under 12 so have not addressed the specific issues for these young witnesses in this book. For teenage and adult witnesses and defendants, I have worked with many types of vulnerability: identified learning disabilities from an early age; late diagnosed autistic spectrum condition; neurological conditions such as Multiple Sclerosis and traumatic brain damage, and a wide range of mental health conditions. For some clients, the identification of their special needs has been clear to all, and has affected their education, adult care and employment opportunities. But this is not the case for everyone.

I met 60-year-old Jim who had worked for most of his life teaching technical skills. In recent years, he had taken up employment as a care assistant and was then accused of aggressive behaviour toward a care home resident. This resident presented with severe Autistic Spectrum Disorder, was mostly non-verbal and had a history of challenging behaviour. Jim's solicitor had made the initial observation that something was awry with Jim's communication, but without a history of special schooling or medical diagnosis, he took the chance of referring him to me. When Jim met me for an assessment, he brought a close friend along. Meeting in the entrance to the office, I was unsure which of them was the vulnerable person. But once we started the assessment, it became clear that Jim would need help in court. He struggled to process verbal information and did not easily recognise non-verbal cues. The court authorised my involvement for the one-day trial hearing in the local magistrates' court. When Jim gave evidence, my recommendations included putting questions at a slow pace and giving him several seconds to compose his response.

When the trial finished and Jim was awaiting the verdict, I sat with him and his friend in the waiting area of the court building. I asked him for some feedback on my involvement. He replied *"I'm 61 and I have always thought I was a bit odd and had trouble talking to people. No-one ever explained why this was. You are the first person who has told me that I am slow at processing and lack understanding of non-verbal and non-literal communication. Whatever the verdict, I have really learned something today!"* The judge found him guilty but gave him a suspended sentence and stated clearly that Jim should never have been allocated to work with such significantly impaired residents.

I met Abe, a 40-year-old man who attended his assessment with his older brother. Throughout the meeting, Abe looked to his brother for advice. Toward the end of the meeting, I explained to his brother that I was concerned about Abe's communication, listed my findings, and said that I would be recommending the involvement of an Intermediary at all his conferences and hearings. I asked if his brother wanted to add anything to my conclusions about Abe's difficulties. His brother's response brought tears to my eyes – which I managed to hide until they left the room. He said that this was the very first time in his life he felt someone had understood Abe.

About three days into a crown court trial, I was assisting Bernard, a 75-year-old man, who had not been assessed by any experts such as a psychologist or psychiatrist, but who I had found in my assessment to have a very poor auditory working memory and ability to process information when it was spoken to him. (He performed much better with written information.) Bernard spontaneously offered this: *"Having your help in this trial has made me realise how I am... the trouble I have concentrating...I did not know before! Just knew that all my life I have always depended on my wife to sort things out".*

I was asked to assess 16-year-old Connor, an alleged victim in a Ministry of Defence court martial. He had been hospitalised following a mental health section earlier in the year, but had improved considerably and was staying with his parents, although quite disengaged from any interaction with them. A psychiatric assessment had given him a diagnosis of Autistic Spectrum Disorder, but when I met him this seemed to be a mild and high functioning type of the condition. Not sleeping was probably his biggest problem. He described himself as *"depressed, no friends and nothing to do"*. His main concern was to be able to wear his beanie hat when he went to court, and I told him confidently that the judge would likely accept such a recommendation. When I left, the soldier who had accompanied me to the house expressed his astonishment at the way I had chatted with Connor and the amount of information I been able to gain. He said it had been so very different from all the other conversations he had observed on other visits to Connor's house.

I do not have special powers, but I am a specialist in communication and that is what I offer to the legal system. Previous therapeutic practice, academic study of communication has led to an approach which after so many years is part of who I am, and difficult to define. Along with my colleagues in the

Intermediary profession, I observe and listen to a huge number of individuals who seem to have slipped by without inviting attention, until they reach the legal system. Most do not have physical handicaps and many pass under the radar at school. They 'look OK'. They also have a life-time practice in avoidance and defence strategies that keep their difficulties under wraps.

The legal system has many assumptions about 'average' and 'normal', often based on the limited diversity of the academically successful and relatively socially protected group of people who become lawyers, and although there is certainly an increase in numbers of women and people from ethnic minorities joining the judiciary compared with 20 years ago, in general many in the legal professions take for granted the level of jargon and complexity of the courtroom.

A new Intermediary observed my work with Max, and said *'I suppose what really hit home today was how Max was able to answer questions when you seriously broke the information down to bite-size chunks and explained simply. He was lost when overloaded - a real example of too much information!'*
The Intermediary brings expertise in communication to share with the experts in legal matters.

****

We can learn a lot from listening and observing communities and cultures different from our own. I have met several people from the travelling community, who have needed to interact with the courts, mostly in the role of defendant, but also as witnesses or alleged victims. I have learned a great deal from them about the assumptions we make every day, that do not take account of people with very different life experiences. This is not unique to travellers, but it helps me to recognise the need to check out expectations for each client.

Rick arrived at court with his aunt for a five-day trial. Rick told me to *"Hurry it all along, as I am only gonna stay for a day…and I'm certainly not coming back again tomorrow"*. When I tried to explain he needed to be there for five days, his aunt took me to one side and said, *"You won't understand, but us travellers have our own ways and we can't fit with yours"*. Many do not grasp the different tones and communication etiquettes required. Another traveller Steve was asked by a judge *"What are you like when you are drunk?"*, to which Steve replied, *"I don't know, your honour, what are you like?"* He told me later he did not mind going to prison as he had heard the local jail had good duvets. Steve had never had his own bed.

When I need to assess and work with a vulnerable witness, a police officer acts as the conduit for the whole process. Almost every police officer I have worked with has been appreciative of the involvement of an Intermediary, even if somewhat frustrated by the long waits for a suitable time to meet. Many have gone out of their way to meet me at local train stations and ensured I am well looked after. That first car journey is often a very useful time for exchanging information about the witness and the needs of the individual case. The officer remains with me throughout the assessment and the rapport between us is essential to providing a smooth service to the witness. After the assessment, I assist the officer in planning the pre-recorded interview with the witness, the pre-trial visits to court and any practical arrangements.

When I work with a defendant, there is no equivalent link person. The solicitor is rarely available in his office, let alone present in the meeting room, although he acts as a vital go-between in communicating with the barrister and the court. When a solicitor does sit in for the assessment, it can be a very useful time for sharing techniques for communicating with the client. This discrepancy will need addressing if /when an Intermediary scheme for defendants is planned by the MoJ.

In every case, I explain the purpose of our assessment meeting, request their consent to continue, and at the end when I have explained my role and how I might be able to assist, I ask if they would like my help, stressing that it is their choice.

One witness, Shona, was clearly linguistically able but with serious trust issues following many admissions to mental health units. She did not want another new person entering her world. She refused my involvement at her interview.

I met Xan, a 16-year-old defendant for the first time with his foster mother. He was resistant to the idea of an Intermediary sitting beside him in court. He was charged with three of his mates and he did not want to stand out as different, or *"stupid"* to the judge. He chose not to have my assistance at court, despite his barrister trying to explain the benefits of understanding the trial.

Back to the GRHs - that vary so much between judges. I have heard a suggestion that once the Intermediary has assisted at this hearing, they should not be required to attend during the cross-examination of a witness. The judge argued that once the questions have been reviewed and written down with the help of the Intermediary, there would be no need to book her for the trial, or a 'section 28' video-recorded cross-examination. This approach fails to recognise the role of the Intermediary in preparing the witness for the court experience. Communication is dynamic and witnesses can be unpredictable. Barristers likewise. I am aware of at least one case where the cross-examining defence barrister accepted all the revisions to his written questions proposed by the Intermediary the day beforehand and then commenced cross-examination completely off-script, leaving the Intermediary with no option but to intervene repeatedly. If she had not been present, the GRH preparation would not have been sufficient.

There is also so much to do before the witness starts being questioned. I often say that if the preparation is thorough, I will not need to intervene, and the witness will be seen as a competent communicator. When Jeremiah finished giving his evidence, the police officers in the case were quick to say, "*he did a lot better than we expected*" and the usher told me "*he really wasn't so special needs was he!*" That is when I know I have done a good job! I have adapted the communication and communication environment so that this vulnerable person is able to communicate effectively.

Before questioning, Intermediaries often recommend that the judge and barristers meet the witness. This meeting, usually in the witness service waiting area, can be very effective in reducing anxiety for the witness.

The waiting period, which can be several hours if not well-managed, and needs careful handling by the Intermediary. During these times, a witness can become so distressed that his evidence is unlikely to be his best.

On one occasion, I was aware that there was some dissent from the defence barrister to an Intermediary being in court with Josie, a very vulnerable alleged victim who suffered frequent hallucinations and flashbacks. The GRH had been short and perfunctory, but there was agreement that the judge and counsel should meet Josie before she came into court. The judge came down to the witness waiting area to meet Josie. I arranged the seating to accommodate Josie's fear of being too close to strangers, and, although the judge was only present for 5-6 minutes, Josie began to hallucinate and I used some strategies to assist her in returning to the real events in the room. When the judge went back into court, she told the defence barrister that she had been convinced of the *"highly specialist skills of the Intermediary which would be essential to Josie's effective communication"*. My report and my contribution to the GRH had not been sufficient – the judge had to see it for herself. Perhaps it is only through real experience that we convince others of our value.

"Asking an Intermediary if she recommends an Intermediary is self-serving"

The MoJ recruits and trains Registered Intermediaries (currently for criminal prosecution witnesses only), and provides a Procedural Guidance Manual and Code of Conduct. Once registered, we are self-employed, independent practitioners, and are expected to manage our own continuing professional development. There is a Quality Assurance Board at the MoJ, but it does not have a Registered Intermediary on its panel.

There are currently around 200 Registered Intermediaries (RIs) in England and Wales. Scotland has its own legal system. Northern Ireland has a separate scheme, run on similar lines, but includes the provision of a service to defendants when they give evidence. Many practitioners work part-time, coordinating the role alongside a related professional practice, such as Speech & Language Therapy, Occupational Therapy, Special Needs Teaching and Psychology.

Registered Intermediaries come to Intermediary work with a range of specialisms and competencies related to types of vulnerability. The scheme asks each practitioner to identify which client groups she can work with. For example, a special needs teacher with experience of Learning Difficulties is unlikely to take a referral for an elderly person who suffered a Stroke, or a deaf person requiring signing. Similarly, although my original basic training as a Speech & Language Therapist qualified me to work with children, I have mostly worked with adults and teenagers in the last 30 years. As a result, my caseload as an Intermediary does not include children. The matching referral service run by the National Crime Agency records each Intermediary's competency ranges and a database matches referred witnesses appropriately. Referrals are made by either the police force or the CPS. The referral rate is around 500 per month at the time of writing, and has been increasing every year since its inception.

Our role is specific and circumscribed. An intermediary is not an expert witness and as such her advice to the court is neutral and cannot be offered as evidence in a case. When Rachel, a young witness, told me that she has occasional flights of delusion as part of her mental illness, I had a duty to include this in my report to the court. However, unless a medical or psychological expert report is filed to support this condition, the defence cannot tell the jury that she has a history of delusional states and use that to suggest that what she witnessed was in her imagination. I met Rachel a few years ago and the mention of 'delusional state' in my report resulted in an adjournment whilst a psychiatric assessment was carried out. The prosecuting counsel was furious with me for, as he saw it, delaying proceedings. As an Intermediary, I had a duty to report what I had been told. The trial took place several months later, and during questioning, Rachel revealed a frequent delusion that she had been on two dates with a famous American pop star. In support of this belief, Rachel wore her favourite t-shirt to court, with a photo image of the same film star across the front. In fact, Rachel had never left her small town in Northern England and had not met this pop star. When she started to talk about the pop star in her evidence, it became clear to the court that her evidence was unreliable. The judge halted the trial and the defendant was released.

An Intermediary is not an emotional supporter. It can be very hard to separate out the role of managing mental health issues to maximise coherent communication and providing emotional support. Most witnesses would like some emotional support when they go into court. Everyone is anxious, as many judges have reminded me. There is plenty of research evidence that the areas of the brain responsible for language and verbal reasoning are significantly compromised by anxiety. If the witness has a phobia of crowded rooms, large open spaces, or moves into a disassociated state when retraumatised, then the Intermediary can help manage the communication environment to achieve best evidence.

Terry reported non-recent (historic) sex abuse to the police. He had experienced both physical and psychological difficulties following the alleged crimes. He had bladder incontinence and required a toilet close by. He lived a long way from the city of his alleged childhood abuse. When calm and in a familiar environment, his communication was competent. He had established a very close relationship with his girlfriend, spending much of his days with her and her family, and when she was beside him, he felt much more confident. During our assessment meeting, she sat silently beside Terry, holding his hand and smiling reassuringly.

I reported to the court that Terry did not need an Intermediary to assist with his communication. However, he needed to be in a live link room, with a toilet next door. His girlfriend could provide the emotional support by sitting beside him holding his hand, faced away to the side, listening to music through headphones so that she could not hear the questions or his responses. The court agreed, and I did not need to attend. However, my assessment and subsequent recommendations had played a significant part in allowing Terry to give evidence.

Ursula was a resident in a secure psychiatric unit. She suffered with extreme anxiety, curling up in a ball away from me when we first met. She experienced inner voices, mostly telling her not to speak to me. She was academically bright, having taken a break from her university course when her mental health deteriorated. The ward staff helped Ursula and I to decide on some strategies for managing her anxiety, including breathing techniques and visual distractors. In the court link room, she sat on the floor for periods of her evidence, sometimes writing her responses for me to read aloud to the court. During the breaks, we used the planned techniques.

I had initially thought that as Ursula was a university student, with no history of special educational needs, she would not need the evidential questions to be adapted in linguistic style or vocabulary. However, on reflection and considering the compromised frontal lobe of a traumatised brain, I viewed the questions of the defence barrister in advance and advised on some changes to simplify and clarify meanings. The court was grateful for her evidence and Ursula was empowered by being able to complete it.

****

Another central aspect of our work is our neutrality. To maintain this, the Procedural Guidance Manual for Registered Intermediaries states that we must not be left alone with a witness. As such we cannot then be compromised in our neutrality by the witness telling us information about the case which would need to be disclosed and turn the Intermediary into an evidential witness. When Vicki told the police officer and I that she had wanted sex but he (the accused) had not been very good at it, and that was why she was accusing him of rape, the officer could report this information. If I had been left alone and had heard this disclosure, I would then have had to stand down as an Intermediary and become a witness. I have been in some courts where the judge has ordered that I am not on view, as if I will in some way affect the jury's opinion of the witness. When we assist a witness in a link room, it is important that we are on full view alongside the witness, so the court can see we are not in any way coaching her in her answers.

This neutrality ensures we can advise the whole court. An Intermediary can view the questions of both defence and prosecution in advance, providing advice to both on the best route to maximise communication. Of course, it can be very hard to change the habits for a barrister after a long professional legal career where articulacy and wide-ranging vocabularies are highly valued. I recall asking a barrister to replace the word '*obtain*' with '*get*', as the former was not in the witness's vocabulary. The barrister replied that he did not mean '*get*', and needed to be more specific in his language. I tried hard to explain that using a word that was not understood was similar to speaking in a foreign language. I believe it is not an easy move, but an essential one that needs to be grasped.

Wilma, a young alleged victim with Learning Difficulties was to be cross-examined, following a video-recording of her evidence. I met with the defence barrister shortly after he had read my report and suggested that we spend some time reviewing his questions to ensure Wilma could understand and respond to the best of her ability. He replied that he preferred to think on his feet when he cross-examined. Anticipating this possible response, as it was not the first time I had heard it, I suggested we discuss some sample question types, and that the more help I could give beforehand, the less likely my interventions would interrupt his flow.

The defence barrister returned to court the following morning and told the judge that he had read some case law which indicated he did not have to "*put his case*" at all, so he was not going to cross-examine Wilma and she would not need to come to court.

'Putting the case', as I have understood it, has traditionally been at the centre of a cross-examination; it is when the advocate challenges the witness about inconsistencies and differences between the witness's evidence and the 'other side'. Intermediaries are not appointed to interfere with this process. The judge holds the reins on the subject or topic of questioning. An Intermediary is there to assist in ensuring that communication is effective in terms of vocabulary and grammar, and to assist the witness to give their best evidence. In many cases, the advocate wants to challenge the witness, by in effect saying that she is lying, in varying degrees of directness. There are indeed circumstances where this would not be sensitive to a young child or a mentally unwell adult. In my experience, many adult witnesses want the opportunity to answer such a question as *"Mr X says this didn't happen, what do you say?"* so that they can emphasise the passion with which they believe their evidence to be true.

The judge may well direct the advocate to present his case through his closing speech to the jury, rather than challenge a fragile witness – I see this happening more frequently and in many cases, it may well be the most appropriate approach. However, for many witnesses, the opportunity to respond to a challenge is an important part of going to court.

Wilma thankfully had not yet started her journey to court and the police officer called her mother and explained she would not be needed. I do not know if this was justice. From the accused's position, I may have wanted the jury to see Wilma and have my barrister *'put my case'*.

****

Let us now look in more detail at the Intermediary availability for criminal defendants in England and Wales. There is no MoJ scheme, no recruitment, matching service or registration as there is for witnesses. In my introduction, I spoke of Naomi Mason, a Registered Intermediary, who responded to an increasing demand for Intermediaries for defendants. In 2011, she set up Communicourt Ltd based in Birmingham at the same time as a similar private company Triangle based in Brighton, and started to recruit Intermediaries and take referrals for vulnerable defendants. The referrals came from solicitors, the funding for assessment from the Legal Aid Agency and the funding for court attendance from HMCTS (7). Over the years the service has expanded to meet an ever-increasing need. Intermediaries at Communicourt are mostly Speech and Language Therapists, employed full time by the company and work almost entirely with defendants. Communicourt and Triangle have a combined referral rate of around 80 per month at time of writing. The recruitment and training process is longer than for Registered Intermediaries, and ongoing supervision, peer support and professional development is more established. However, as the MoJ states, there is no recognised national registration of Intermediaries working with defendants, and as such it is unregulated and non-registered. There has been much criticism of the private company provision, but it has filled a void where the state has yet to set up a service to meet the needs of a vulnerable population.

On referral, Intermediaries assess the client. The assessment has three main purposes: to evaluate the communication skills of the client, decide if an Intermediary could make a difference and make recommendations for how that difference can be effected. "Self-serving and ridiculous" (see the title of this chapter) was how one judge evaluated the idea of an Intermediary assessing and deciding if a defendant needed an Intermediary. I understand why he might think that, particularly when I have been told that there is an inflated perception of our fees. However, there are two aspects to the counter-argument.

Firstly, the referral rate for Intermediaries to assist defendants is at least twice as many as the number of trained Intermediaries available to take on their cases. I receive at least two requests every day for my service. Each defendant needs a minimum of two days of my time (and perhaps a maximum of 30 days) to provide the service required. I often need a full day to assess, as there are hours of travelling or the defendant is on remand, and it is time consuming getting into a prison for a legal visit. I need several hours to prepare a report, read any psychology and psychiatry reports, and another day minimum to attend court. Clearly, I do not have enough days in my week to meet this demand.

Communicourt reports a six-week waiting time from referral to assessment, and at time of writing was turning away nearly half of all referrals due to lack of capacity (8). The Intermediaries for Justice organisation, set up in 2015 as a professional body for all Intermediaries, has a database of independent Intermediaries (mostly Registered Intermediaries) who will take defendant cases. They receive around 60 referrals a month, many unfilled.

With this state of play, it is clearly not necessary to recommend the involvement of an Intermediary in a defendant's trial for our own monetary gain. We have more than enough work and there is considerable stress in responding to referrers with the news that we cannot hope to take on their client in the foreseeable future as our diaries are so full. When I receive a call from a solicitor looking for an Intermediary for a five week murder trial starting in 6 days, and I anticipate the probable national lack of availability, I am very sad.

The second aspect to consider in whether we are *"self-serving and ridiculous"* is the general pattern that has existed for most established professions related to health: for example, physiotherapists, occupational therapists, speech & language therapists. All initial assessments aim to firstly establish if this client is someone for whom we have something to offer, if the needs of the client match our competencies. In the Intermediary assessment, we have firstly to establish the level of communication skills of the defendant, and then, if any adaptation or the involvement of the Intermediary can be recommended to maximise their communication effectiveness.

When I was at Communicourt, and I understand this has not changed, we trained Intermediaries to assess with three possible outcomes: that the defendant was able to manage without an Intermediary as he did not want our help or had sufficient communication skills; that the defendant was too low functioning to benefit from any assistance in real time; and thirdly that an

Intermediary would be beneficial. I will address all three situations in detail.

I have met several defendants, who may be vulnerable in their emotional regulation and were clearly distressed at being charged with crimes, but who had competent communication and therefore did not require the assistance of an Intermediary. My resulting report was sent to the referring solicitor, who would then in most eventualities not need to raise any request for an Intermediary before a judge. As a result, judges do not see Intermediary reports that do not recommend our involvement. Perhaps this may be the reason some judges think we recommend our services in every case!

Zen was referred for assessment. He was working and supporting his family, and had migrated from a non-English speaking country ten years ago. He had completed professional exams in this country and, although he was clearly still more proficient in his first language, he spoke English well. He needed some help in understanding the English legal system, but showed an ability to ask for clarification and understand his advocate at court. I duly wrote a report explaining that he would not need an Intermediary.

I visited three elderly witnesses in their supported living home with a police officer. There had been a report of a temporary member of staff being verbally abusive to residents. All three gentlemen were over 80 and had required 24 hr support throughout their lives. The advantage of an Intermediary assessment for the police officer, was that I could ascertain their communication abilities without discussing the case and help the officer with best ways to get their evidence. All three men were not able to recall consistently any events in their recent life and one man could not stay awake long enough to be assessed. The case could not proceed without their evidence, aa the permanent care staff had not been witnesses to the alleged incidents. My involvement saved the legal system financially in this case, although of course the crime was not solved. The judges would not have seen this report.

Sometimes my assessment conclusions do not match the actual needs of the client once we get to court. I may have concluded that a defendant or witness requires the assistance of an Intermediary, and during the trial it becomes obvious that he is less vulnerable and a better communicator. There may be several reasons for this.

Sharon was a more able communicator in court when evidence was about real people and events in her life. She knew all the people involved, she had given her evidence to police in a video interview suite, and with the support of the witness service volunteers who helped her settle in the court building, was well able to respond to questions that followed the ground rules authorised by the judge. She did not need an Intermediary with her when she was cross-examined. In such a situation, the Intermediary input prior to her attendance at court was more valuable, and had a significant effect on Sharon's experience of court and her ability to give clear evidence.

In another situation, the witness may have been more vulnerable at the time of the assessment, but by the time she attended court, her mental health had improved. Mental health is not consistent and can be affected both positively and negatively by many factors. Thomasina had received a supportive letter from her boyfriend the day before the trial and was feeling confident. Irwin liked the rules and structure of the formal crown court, as he felt it fitted with his obsessive-compulsive tendencies. If the timings of the court were clear for him, he did not need an Intermediary. Vaz's doctor prescribed an increase in his medication two weeks before his trial, which made him more able to manage his anxiety and panic attacks. Yuval took a trip home to his family for several months before the trial. His mental health improved considerably as a result and so he did not need my help.

There will also be situations where the Intermediary gets an unrealistic picture of the client's abilities. When I first assessed William, I was very concerned about his extreme anxiety and inability to focus on any new information, even in the relaxed environment of a small interview room. I reported that he would need assistance at his trial. However, when I arrived at the court, I noted that he had made copious notes on his case (where previously he had described himself as dyslexic and struggling to write independently). I cannot say for sure whether he had deliberately misled me during assessment. However, it was apparent to me that he was very competent and aware of the details of his case during the two days I attended his trial. I had originally been asked to assist just for his giving of evidence, but as the trial was late in starting, I was in court well before his evidence was due. By the time William was called to the witness box, I had changed my view of his abilities and agreed with the judge that he did not require my assistance.

I think both judges and barristers have some concern that witnesses and defendants will play on the Intermediary's supposed naivety about crime. They believe that a defendant will convince us of their vulnerability if he believes it might assist their case. I have mentioned that many defendants have also been victims of some sort during their lives and so self-protective strategies will most likely be strong. The flip side of this is that most defendants are anxious not to be considered weak, '*delinquent*' as one man told me, or stupid. The involvement of an Intermediary may increase this anxiety.

Back to my three possible outcomes of an Intermediary assessment. The second possible outcome is that even with all the skills of an experienced Intermediary, this defendant will not manage to participate effectively in his trial. In these situations, it is often poor retention of even a simple short piece of information, and poor consistency in responding 'yes' or 'no' to concrete questions, that leads to such a conclusion. When this recommendation is relayed to the court, some judges request that we should '*come along anyway*' as the defendant has been deemed fit to plead. This is a difficult situation where the Intermediary is perhaps being used as the sticking plaster that will allow the court to say the defendant had sufficient support to participate effectively.

In such cases, I have attended the trial, and then had to address the judge after the first day to indicate that the defendant was not getting any benefit from my presence. However simply I explained the proceedings, he was unable to retain the information. Sometimes, the court has then adjourned to seek psychiatric reports on 'fitness to plead'.

At the Communicourt agency, 24% of all assessments conclude that an Intermediary is not recommended. This is split between those who are sufficiently competent to manage without, and those who are so poor at understanding and communicating that an Intermediary could not make a significant difference.

When I assessed Amy, I wrote a report concluding that she was not going to be able to participate effectively even with an Intermediary. There were no recommendations in the report, as I did not believe there were any adaptations which would be sufficiently effective. The judge asked me to attend. On the first day of the trial, the CPS dropped the case, although I do not know if this was related to the Intermediary's conclusions or presence.

In another case, Sylvia was a defendant with a recently diagnosed type of brain damage that was affecting her recall of her actions in both the recent and historic past. She told me that since retiring from her professional life, she had started to have unexplained brief episodes of loss of consciousness, which were in themselves very frightening. She described how, for example, she had travelled to Africa on holiday, but on her return, she did not recall any of the trip. If a friend told Sylvia that she had been to Africa, she believed her but could not recall any of the experience. On a day to day basis, still living alone, she had implemented strategies such as visual lists and audio reminders and was managing to continue to live alone, but Sylvia was consciously fearful of her deteriorating situation. The Psychology report confirmed a neuropathological progressive condition.

In my report to the court, I described this phenomenon and indicated how this would impact on the trial, in which she was charged with a non-recent abuse. The case was dropped. It seemed to me that although the CPS had read the diagnosis, until an Intermediary itemised the adaptations and limitations that would present themselves in the practicality of a trial, the CPS had not fully appreciated Sylvia's medical condition.

Back to the three possible outcomes of an Intermediary assessment. The third possible recommendation is that the defendant would benefit from an Intermediary for their trial. These are the reports the judges see and so will give the impression we always recommend our involvement.

While this impression remains, many courts require an expert report from a psychologist or psychiatrist to determine whether an Intermediary is recommended. In my experience in some cases, this can be a costly, time-consuming and ineffective use of expert advice. If I go back to my NHS experience, it is like the doctor deciding whether speech therapy is required, when the speech therapist needed to reach her own conclusion on whether she could offer effective interventions. In the legal sphere, I find some expert reports do not fully appreciate the role of the Intermediary, or they try to define the specific recommendations of the Intermediary assessment. It can be a difficult situation when the psychiatrist recommends an Intermediary, and then I conclude I cannot make an effective contribution.

The Lord Chief Justice issued Criminal Practice Directions in April 2016 that the appointment of an Intermediary for a defendant giving evidence would be *'rare'* and for the entire trial *'extremely rare'* (14). I do not know how 'rare' is defined. This judgement is based on barristers and judges being competent to adapt their communication to the needs of each vulnerable individual, and family members being able to sit beside some vulnerable defendants and explain the processes of the court trial; this is not my experience.

There has been some significant compliance with this direction from judges across the country. I heard recently of a crown court where judges had been told not to permit an Intermediary for any defendant case at all. I am confused as to how this allows for the judge to use his inherent powers to ensure effective participation of vulnerable people. In other courts, judges have recognised that *'rare'* does not mean *'never'*.

On figures obtained from the MoJ website, there were 400,000 crown and magistrates court criminal cases during the last three months of 2016. During that time, it is likely that no more than 350 defendants were assisted by Intermediaries from a combination of Communicourt, Triangle and Intermediaries for

Justice referrals. This amounts to less 0.1% of all cases, which I would define as 'extremely rare'. Does this indicate that the Lord Chief Justice wants courts to continue to use Intermediaries at the current level?

When I started looking at statistics from the MoJ, I came across some other interesting figures. During the same three months of 2016, over 38,000 requests were made for interpreters or translators. I have been thinking about the level of understanding of some of the defendants where the judge has refused the appointment of an Intermediary. If these defendants had English as a second language, and they were proficient in their first language, there would have been an application for an interpreter. Does this mean that being a non-English speaker makes you more likely to be recognised as vulnerable than an English speaker with special needs? To further complicate this, some of our bilingual clients are not proficient in either language, most likely because of a cognitive impairment. Then the Intermediary may need to request an interpreter to work with the Intermediary. Again, this can be less straight forward than first observed.

Benyamin had lived in London all his adult life, living with his family who spoke Hindi at home. He had been diagnosed with Learning Difficulties. Initially the solicitor assumed he would need an interpreter. When I met Benyamin, he told me he preferred to speak in English, and if I simplified my vocabulary and grammar, he was competent in that language. This was certainly less time consuming and less costly than involving an interpreter as well.

There is an assumption that the first step in providing a national Intermediary scheme to defendants will be to ensure they have assistance with giving evidence. Of course, this initially seems like the most active part of the trial for a defendant, as it is the only time they are asked to speak during their trial. Answering questions in front of a large audience, particularly cross-examination which is intended to challenge their assumption of innocence, is certainly daunting and complex for someone with poor communication skills.

If this was the only part the defendant needed to play, he could be asked to attend just when he was needed in the witness box. However, the defendant is required to attend the whole trial, sit in the court and as such participate effectively.

I believe that effective participation includes understanding the evidence against him, talking productively with his counsel in conferences outside the court, and being able to read the documents set out for the jury.

When the time comes to decide whether to give evidence (and the defendant always has a choice), the verbal reasoning involved will often be a struggle for many vulnerable defendants.

It cannot be a fair system that requires a defendant to attend a trial which, for all intents and purposes, is experienced as a partly-understood foreign language, and then expects him to answer questions that often relate back to evidence he has not fully understood.

It is also not straight forward to suggest that if a defendant needs any help, it will be at the stage of giving evidence in the first instance. That would be a simple conclusion, and true for those with just a speech impediment and good language comprehension. But it has certainly not always been my experience.

Chris had been diagnosed with Autistic Spectrum Disorder at an early age. He had been home-schooled since the age of 13, as a placement could not be found to meet his behavioural difficulties. His parents were initially pleased that he had found some employment in a kitchen at the age of 16, but when Chris realised that the presence of sharp implements encouraged his self-harming, he had resigned from his job. The local community mental health services were not able to engage with him as he could not cope with their group sessions, and his psychiatrist prescribed anti-psychotic and anti-depressants to manage his low mood and frequent outbursts. This lack of emotional regulation was key to the criminal charges which included assault and public order offences.

On initial assessment, another Intermediary assessed his linguistic abilities and recommended that he have the assistance of an Intermediary for the whole trial. When the District Judge read the report, he intimated that perhaps he would allow assistance for evidence, but not for the whole trial. The assessing Intermediary replied that she would not be able to assist on this limited basis. I have on many occasions responded similarly and there are good reasons for this approach.

The case was to be heard in a magistrates' court with a time limit of one day. When the request went out nationally for an Intermediary to assist for 'giving evidence only', I was the only person to respond. I wrote to the referring court saying that, in effect in such a short trial, by the time the Intermediary had attended a GRH at the beginning of the day, carried out some essential practice with the defendant to orient him to the witness box, and read case papers so she was familiar with the context of the case, and then assisted with evidence, there would be little difference in costs for the court to have the Intermediary present for the whole day's trial.

I received a reply from the court asking me to attend a GRH the week before the trial listing. I was surprised at this, as this additional attendance would certainly increase the costs. However, when I mentioned this to the court listings officer, she replied that the District Judge required my presence on that earlier date, and so of course I attended.

I mentioned also that as part of my code of ethics and practice (set for registered Intermediaries but adhered to in defendant cases as there is no alternative code) I would need to read the initial Intermediary report and meet the defendant for up to an hour to review the findings and conclude my own recommendations. This is where the case became unusual.

I attended court for a GRH. As explained previously, this type of hearing was introduced to allow special measures and specific ground rules relating to a vulnerable child or adult to be discussed between the judge, advocates and Intermediary, using the Intermediary's report as the basis of the discussion. In this case however, the hearing was used to contest the appointment of an Intermediary. I received a copy of the previous Intermediary's report, and was surprised to read that Chris' linguistic abilities, in both understanding and expressing himself were well above the population of vulnerable defendants I generally assist. He was however more affected by his mental health issues on the day of the trial. When I met with Chris early on the day of the hearing, he lacked the ability to focus and attend to complex legal arguments and make decisions with full understanding. He rarely indicated his lack of comprehension and, importantly, his parents struggled also to grasp the full meaning. They could not be depended on to explain the court proceedings by sitting beside him. I concluded that he would benefit from Intermediary assistance in focussing, attending and understanding the complexity of his case, his decision on whether to plead guilty or not, and ensuring full comprehension of the process of the trial. However, I did not think Chris needed assistance with responding to specific questions in giving evidence as his linguistic skills were competent.

I entered the courtroom, expecting to give a verbal report to the judge on my findings. He was well versed in the recent case law and the Lord Chief Justice's Criminal Practice Direction. He was therefore surprised by my conclusions. He suggested that a family member could assist in the dock, and was not easily persuaded that there were any specialist skills required in the work I envisaged doing as an Intermediary. I explained that Chris's mother was clearly unable to assist, as she had shown considerable confusion about the court process during my assessment that morning.

The judge asked me to inform the court of the additional cost of staying for both parts of the trial, and when I offered to keep the costs equal, he agreed to my recommendations. This observation added to my belief that costs are often upper-most in the minds of those trying to limit our involvement for more than the giving of evidence.

I decided to write an addendum report to the court, with a brief outline of my findings and recommendations. The judge had been insistent that he did not want a written report of my review assessment, no doubt again with concern for costs. However, I realised as I left the court that the trial was to be heard in front of a magistrates' bench (that is not with the same judge), with a different prosecutor and potentially a different defence advocate from the one who had attended the 'GRH'. I wanted to be sure the bench was alerted to the purposes of my attendance.

On the morning of the trial, I sat with Chris when he met with his solicitor. The solicitor had a slow delivery of speech and had somewhat simplified his explanations. However, when I checked for understanding, it was clear that Chris had only grasped a small proportion of what had been said. When the solicitor read the prosecution witness statements aloud, the language was too complex. Those sections Chris did understand, just raised his stress levels and he became quite aggressive in his demeanour and responses. The witness statements described how he had held his girlfriend by the throat, hit out at a passer-by and caused injury to them. Chris struggled to accept that there were two sides in a trial and that both explanations would need to be told to the court.

The solicitor then explained how the evidence was strong against Chris and, particularly as two of the witnesses were passers-by with professional backgrounds, the magistrates might well believe them. He very fairly advised on both sides of the argument, the consequences of pleading guilty at this stage compared with taking the risk of a trial and then being found guilty. I drew a simple flow diagram with the two options of entering guilty or not guilty pleas, as the solicitor progressed in his explanation.

The solicitor left the room to speak with prosecution about a plea and prepare a written 'basis' for this plea. The parents immediately turned to me and thanked me for my explanations. They said they had not understood the solicitor as he had used language they did not understand, and it was clear that Chris was also confused. I referred them back to the flow diagram I had drawn. Chris initially said he could not plead guilty to something he did not do, but started to understand the implications of being a young person with a 'referral order' which does not create a criminal record which would affect his employment chances for the immediate future. He expressed how important it was to get his job back and decided to plead guilty.

When the solicitor returned with a written statement or 'basis' (the word he used and which Chris did not understand), I asked if I could read it aloud to Chris. There were several words that he did not understand such as *'facilitated'* and *'inappropriate'*. I simplified these and then the solicitor rewrote the statement.

In court, I explained to the legal advisor before the magistrates entered, that on a pre-trial visit to the court during the previous week, Chris had preferred to sit in the dock (which was at right angles to the seating of the lawyers), as he was able to see the advocates' faces when they spoke, and I could whisper to him with less disturbance during the proceedings. My request for him to have a large ball of Blue Tack as a distractor was recommended and accepted.

The hearing took less than an hour as his guilty plea meant a trial was not needed, and the defendant was able to effectively participate in his case. I wrote a simplified summary list of the magistrates' deliberations and went through it with him and his parents when we left court.

As I left the court, the magistrate thanked me and said that *"I hadn't been needed in the end as there wasn't a trial"*. Clearly the assumption of the bench was that an Intermediary was required only when a defendant was questioned. Chris would not have reached his conclusion on a plea without my assistance – that is my honest belief. Giving evidence is only a small part of participating effectively in a trial.

Before moving on, I should address a recent judicial suggestion that 'just about anyone' could sit beside a defendant to explain the proceedings and that the skills of an Intermediary were not required during most of the trial process. I have yet to meet a relative or friend of a vulnerable defendant who understands the legal process sufficiently to carry out this role. When a person is vulnerable, he needs assurance and information. The professionals in the courtroom assume a lot of knowledge about how trials work and the rules of the court. And it is not sufficient to tell a vulnerable defendant in a conference room just before the trial starts and expect him to process and recall the information. This is the whole point of the defendant's vulnerability – he cannot retain or utilise information and does not know what he has not understood. I observed an extreme form of this when Connor's mother told me: *"I have told Connor to watch Judge Judy...that will help him understand the court we are going to"*. Judge Judy and a Magistrates Court have very little in common. Watching American court dramas has a similar disadvantage. It takes a skilled Intermediary with a good knowledge of court processes to adequately signpost the vulnerable person. Maybe this is another situation where we need to compare the interpreter and Intermediary services. Family members are not asked to interpret for a defendant – the court pays for an interpreter.

In another case, Natasha was the alleged victim called to court to be cross-examined. On the morning of the trial, the defendant changed his plea to guilty on a limited basis. The prosecutor needed to check that Natasha would accept this plea agreement. I was involved in using visual aids and simplifying the explanation so that Natasha could make an informed decision.

Negotiating a guilty plea can be complex. Many people have stumbled trying to explain a *"30% reduction"* in a sentence to a functionally innumerate and illiterate defendant, who just wants to get out of court as quickly as possible. An Intermediary is skilled in simplifying the language. I often use counters or coins to show the length of sentence, and I then remove a third of them to show the reduction. This usually works.

It is not just the vulnerable who would benefit from simplification of language in court. The general public is clearly confused by Legalise. Legal professionals know they use jargon, but often do not realise quite how much of their speech is specific to their field. I met a solicitor who told a young man with Learning Difficulties, that *"the court was minded to adjourn the case and so it may be re-listed"*. He was surprised when I then simplified this, to *"they might stop today and get another date"*. I appreciate the struggle for a legal professional who has spent all his / her career fine-tuning vocabulary to precision, only to be told to speak simply.

I recently sat with a defendant in a pre-trial conference and noted down some examples of language used by a barrister that would be too complex for most of the people I assist. I thought the reader might like to see these examples:

- *reprehensible behaviour;*

- *past convictions;*

- *binding the hands;*

- *get house in order;*

- *push button;*

- *collateral issue;*

- *butter wouldn't melt;*

- *factual matrix;*

- *fallible;*

- *cut and dry;*

- *mother of all arguments;*

- *contamination;*

- *lie of the land;*

- *highjack issues;*

- *all hell broke loose.*

Simplifying such phrases in real time during a long court session can be difficult for even the most experienced Intermediary, and is certainly not part of many family members' skills.

When I was a student Speech Therapist many years ago: a mother of a small child told me *"I don't like the way the doctor keeps talking about 'developmental problems' – 'develop' is fine but 'mental' doesn't sound right in the head!"* We cannot assume others understand our words.

There are vulnerable defendants who would plead guilty rather than endure a trial. Henry was charged with sexual abuse of a four-year-old child. I met him at court with his barrister on the first day of his eight-day trial, in the court cells as he had been on remand for several months. Henry had a history of petty crimes and told me that when he had previously attended court, he had understood very little and was not able to read any case papers. When I asked him how he had got through the trial, he said '*I put my head down and wait for the judge to sentence me*'. This was the first trial where he had been offered the assistance of an Intermediary. He explained to his barrister that he would rather plead guilty immediately than sit for eight days in the dock. She asked Henry if he had abused the child and he was insistent that he had not. She explained that the sentence was likely to be around 13 years and we talked through the opportunity he would have to give evidence with my help. We discussed his fear of speaking to the court and I explained that we could have a 'practice run' with neutral questions unrelated to the case when the courtroom was empty. We discussed how I was going to sit beside him in the dock and explain the proceedings, and ask for breaks if needed. Henry agreed to continue with the trial, with his not-guilty plea, and gave evidence with my help. The jury acquitted him. Active participation is key to justice.

I think there is an issue here related to delayed gratification. I believe that one of the key characteristics of successful people (in relationships and in work) is delayed gratification: in other words knowing that it is worth putting up with lots of stress and difficulty in the moment, to make a potential gain in the future. Henry, like many other vulnerable defendants I have met, struggled to see the long-term benefit of sticking with the misery of eight days in a dock, and just wanted any quick fix to take him out of court even if it was not fair.

Every defendant has a right to decide whether he gives evidence. The jury can, and will, have an opinion about the reasons for a defendant deciding not to give evidence – perhaps he has something to hide? – and the judge can advise the jury as to whether this decision should be held against him. The decision to give evidence can be dependent on the attitude of the defence barrister. When Ishmael had such poor speech and it was not clear how he would respond to questions, the barrister did not want to take a chance on Ishmael to give evidence. With my assistance, the questions were simplified, and I repeated any less intelligible phrases for the court. Ishmael had his chance to tell the court his side of the story. At Communicourt, based on a caseload of 450 defendants assisted by an Intermediary, around 45% opted to give evidence. I do not know how this compares with the general defendant population or with vulnerable defendants who do not have an Intermediary at their trial. In my view, the presence of an Intermediary increases the likelihood of a defendant choosing to answer questions. This can only be a good thing. If you are to be convicted, knowing you had a chance to speak to the jury or magistrates, must be worthwhile. If you are acquitted, it will be good to know you may have influenced the jury or the magistrates with your words. In such situations, the Intermediary can be an empowering addition to the court process for the vulnerable person.

****

Sometimes I struggle to know how much to challenge inconsistency from the court. I attended a crown court with a defendant called Penelope, but on the first day of the trial after a GRH, we were moved to another court and judge.

The first and second judge had very different approaches to the involvement of an Intermediary. With the first judge, almost all my recommendations were accepted, and when one counsel challenged my advice, I was permitted to explain my reasoning and my advice was accepted by the judge. I left the court feeling valued and appreciated in my role and able to effectively support the defendant.

When the second judge took up the case, he challenged my presence and revoked some of my recommendations without allowing any discussion. The judge stated that he was *"perfectly able to recognise inappropriate questions"* and would make that decision himself, making it clear he would not have authorised my involvement if he had been the judge at earlier hearings.

There can be a fine line in being assertive in this role. In the Registered Intermediary Online discussions, there have been queries on occasion from practitioners asking where it is possible to challenge a judge's decision after it had been made. The judge's decision is final, and as I learned from many advocates, a really useful phrase to adopt when the judge disagrees is *"so be it"*. A very wise Intermediary told me once, it is important to *'move on'* after such a decision. Over-analysing and stewing does not help anyone. Intermediaries advise, judges decide.

In Penelope's case, I was close to challenging the judge when told that I would not be able to intervene directly with counsel during questioning. After all, the previous judge had agreed to this plan. In the split-second I had to consider my response, I chose to say, *'Yes your Honour'*. Both prosecution and defence advocates told me afterward that I had made the right choice, as they had more experience with this judge and did not think it helped to challenge him. Of course, a roaming Intermediary does not know the local judges as well as the advocates.

'Roaming', 'itinerant' or just a 'traveller' might be a good description of the way I have chosen to carry out this Intermediary role. It does not suit everyone, and would not have suited me at a different stage in my life. For the most part, I enjoy the lack of routine and the variety of ways I can make the most of the long train journeys.

This way of working has its challenges. I arrived at a town hall one lunchtime, having been told by the referring solicitor that an interview room had been booked for me, as the most suitable place to see Vic, a respondent in a family case, who had mobility limitations. When I asked at reception, they had my booking but expected me to know the code for getting into the interview room. I did not. Eventually a helpful administrator opened the room for me. It was a secure room, with a long table fixed to the wall on both sides, with an entrance for the client through one door, and the interviewer through a door on the opposite side. At the end of the assessment, I realised that Vic and his wife could leave without any problem. I was however stuck. The door behind me was locked and I had no code or fob. After a few seconds of mild panic, I climbed over the desk and left by the client door!

Yvette was asked to give evidence as a witness in a drugs case. She was a very vulnerable young woman who had previously been arrested but not charged in another case. She had been diagnosed as suffering from Post-Traumatic Stress Disorder, and had attempted suicide twice, most recently just 4 days before the trial. When I arrived at court for a GRH on the first day of the trial, the defence team were contesting my involvement. Their main issue was that the jury would be prejudiced by the presence of an Intermediary. They argued that Yvette had managed to be interviewed by police quite competently, so would not need help in court. I explained the different communication demands of a police interview suite environment compared with a courtroom. The barrister mentioned that he had never seen an Intermediary report that did not recommend their services. Luckily the judge put him right, reminding the barrister that the Intermediary is asked to advise the court as a neutral specialist in communication.

When Amy's case came to court, the barristers were supportive of the involvement of an Intermediary. When I was booked for a GRH, I did not expect to find that my role would be contested by the judge. He concluded that, despite my recommendations about Amy's poor auditory processing of language, she should only have assistance when she gave evidence. As it was a four-day trial, I was asked to attend for the third day to allow me to carry out preparation of questions with barristers and gain a sense of context. The judge said I was not to sit with Amy during the court process as it would give *"an adverse impression"* to the jury, but to join her when she went into the witness box. On day two of the trial, as I was about to start a long journey to the court, I called to check on progress of the trial. Everything was moving slower than expected and Amy was not expected to give evidence until the fourth listed day. I was told to come along anyway and the judge confirmed I could be in court. When I arrived, I discovered that the trial judge had changed, and this judge took a very different view of my involvement. He agreed I could sit beside Amy, and said that I should be allowed to use my *"professional judgement"*. This is core to the stress of working as an Intermediary – the inconsistency of the court perception of the neutrality of my role.

Arriving on the second day of the trial was confusing. I did not know the names of the main protagonists, had not fully understood the charges or heard the prosecutor's opening speech. In conference, I struggled a little to keep up with the discussions, particularly as Amy was cognitively able, but with diagnosed ADHD and extreme anxiety, she did not focus well on one point at a time. This was certainly a case where I found myself re-evaluating the recommendation of an Intermediary. When focussed on her case, she was almost obsessive in her attention and did not need any help from me. When she tried out the witness box in a court adjournment, Amy told me that she would prefer it if I sat away from her, as she did not want the jury to think she was *'stupid'*. She managed with all the questions and I did not need to intervene. I wrote a note to the judge after the trial explaining that with hindsight, this defendant had not needed an Intermediary. I was told he had commented that he would like to discuss the matter, but to date I have not heard from him.

"How can you sit next to a murderer...and help him?"

I have worked with Emily on four cases to date. She has a history of Learning Difficulties, Schizophrenia and Post-Traumatic Stress Disorder. When we first met, I recognised how easy it was to like her and get close to her. It was almost as if she drew you in. She was 20 years old and bubbling with enthusiasm to meet new people. I soon realised this trait drew her into some high-risk situations. She had attachment issues that related to her early years in an abusive environment but had been fostered for most of her childhood. Many vulnerable witnesses give their initial evidence in a video-recorded interview, known colloquially as an ABE (Achieving Best Evidence). Our initial meeting was after Emily had given her evidence. We agreed that she would benefit from my involvement in her preparations for and attendance at court for cross-examination.

In the past, judges have expected witnesses to watch their ABE interview along with the court. Many courts now accept intermediary recommendations for a witness to view this recording at a separate time, in private. I recommend that to minimise the level of re-traumatisation caused by watching oneself talk about this most difficult event, that the vulnerable person watches it at a different time, with time for breaks if the witness becomes distressed. I usually bring along a 9" DVD player with a lid that closes down, so that the witness does not have to view themselves on a large monitor, and can in fact just listen if they prefer. I have noticed that both men and women can be very uncomfortable viewing their younger self, perhaps two years prior to the trial. I also recommend this approach if I anticipate the breaks will also interfere with continuity and timing for the court. In preparation for attending court, Emily needed to refresh her memory on the evidence she had given over a year prior to the trial date. The police officer and I planned to show Emily the recorded interview on the morning of the first day of the trial, away from the court in the neighbouring police station. When we picked up Emily from her home, she sat with me in the back seat and was chatty but nervous about the day ahead.

During the playing of the DVD she became quite distressed, began to hear voices and on two occasions had to stop the DVD whilst she and I did some grounding techniques which we had been practising. Grounding techniques can help to orientate away from abstract to concrete, to focus on the present moment, and Emily was particularly helped by focussing on the colours in the room, and focus on her sense of smell and taste. This was one of my first experiences of the hugely re-traumatising effect of viewing oneself, possibly two years previous, talking about a highly traumatic event. I discussed with the police officer whether it was in Emily's best interests to continue with the viewing. I have since been advised by a judge that the court could not insist on a witness reviewing her DVD. The judge went on to explain that when a witness is given a written statement to review, there was no way of checking if the witness had read it, so similarly a DVD did not have to be watched.

The officer took Emily out for a break and I went into the courtroom to check on progress in the first stages of the trial. I was surprised to find that the trial was being adjourned. The barrister explained that an issue had been raised by the defence that the defendant may be in early stages of dementia and perhaps may not be deemed fit to be tried. The trial was postponed for another four months while a psychiatric assessment of the defendant was arranged.

I realised then that Emily had been shown the DVD unnecessarily. I felt that we had abused her in some way, although I realised it was unintentional. I discussed this with the police officer and she helped me to recognise that we could not predict or mitigate for all circumstances.

Four months later the trial went ahead after the defendant was deemed fit to plead. Emily struggled with her inner voices for some parts of the cross-examination. She elected to be behind a screen in the witness box, rather than on a live link. As a result, whenever I observed that she was being distracted into conversations with her voices, I indicated to the judge and we took a break. When the questioning finished, she was elated and proud of herself. I said goodbye as that was the end of my involvement, and told her that I really hoped, in the nicest possible way, that we would not meet again.

I was truly surprised to receive a referral a year later to assist a different police officer to take evidence from Emily in a new case. I went with the officer to pick Emily up from her home and drive to the interview suite. Sitting in the back seat of the car, I can carry out a great deal of my assessment and establish rapport, while the witness is more relaxed and the informal conversation can be quite revealing of her functional communication.

On this occasion, I was just starting to listen to Emily update me on her life since we last met. She quickly said to me *"Paula, I don't want to do this"*. Further exploration revealed that she wanted to tell the police about what had happened to her, but not on a video-recording. She had struggled with the previous case, could not articulate exactly what she had found difficult, but I was reminded of how the 'memory refresh' (viewing the pre-recorded interview) had evoked a psychotic episode.

I spoke with the interviewing officer and we suggested a written statement in lieu of the video-recorded interview. Emily agreed and seemed relieved. It took three long sessions to complete her evidence in this way. The officer questioned, typed or wrote, whilst I helped Emily to re-focus, to take breaks, confirmed her understanding of the questions and produced a visual aid of a timeline which helped her relate the chronology of the incident. Although both cases related to physical and sexual abuse, the completed trial was several years before and this evidence was about recent experience.

I started to notice how the witness was very keen to prolong each session; perhaps being in the company of two friendly non-judgemental older women was preferable to her current home life.

Initially the officer tried handwriting, and then later typing directly onto computer to see if this would speed up the process.

Unfortunately, before this case could come to court, Emily reported another two alleged incidents and we continued to meet to obtain written evidence. Before we started working on the events of the most recent abuse, I reminded her that with written statements the time in court would increase, maybe double, as examination-in-chief by the prosecutor to set out all the allegations would be necessary as well as cross-examination by defence. She still chose to continue with a written statement over video-recording.

I noticed also that Emily chose to assign to me the role of listener during the statement session. The officer was often not facing her directly, as she was looking at her notepad or laptop screen. So, Emily would speak directly to me, telling me the events, often with prolonged eye contact.

She became concerned at one stage about how I might cope with hearing some quite explicit sexual details. She asked me how many cases I had dealt with and whether hers was the worst. Of course, I did not give her specific answers to this. She said she was worried about how I managed to get it all out of my head. It was interesting that Emily was showing empathy for me, but I also wondered if I was being manipulated.

I did not admit to her that her voice stayed in my head for several hours after each meeting. She had some specific mannerisms that I recognised in others, and I started to wonder about the effect these long sessions and continued involvement with this witness was having on me. Most witnesses require much less of my time, and over a shorter period. By this stage I had known Emily for more than two years and had spent several days with her.

There is plenty of research published on the vicarious or secondary trauma experienced by professionals working in therapeutic and caring roles. Emily did indeed describe some graphic details which were hard to hear.

Emily was desperate for cigarettes and rarely had any of her own. Neither the officer nor I smoked. Emily started to leave the police station during each break and to approach passers-by in the street in the hope that one would give her a cigarette. This was clearly making her additionally vulnerable, when she was supposedly in the safe hands of the police. For the next meeting, I brought some cigarettes and a lighter. I similarly brought sandwiches for lunch to ensure the session could progress without Emily asking for a trip to MacDonald's.

Was I grooming her to give evidence? Was I capitulating and encouraging her to smoke? I discussed this with the police officer. We were both aware that Emily was enjoying our company and looked forward to our meetings. The officer thought my actions were helpful and enabling, so that the sessions could be more concise. I told myself this was all within my role of maximising communication. The role of Intermediary, like many other professions, is an art not a science. I think if I had the time again, I would do the same, but I have not encountered a similar situation since, and of course every case is unique.

None of Emily's cases have yet progressed to trial. Meanwhile Emily's mental health and general stability has deteriorated. She is involved with drugs and has been accused of theft. Back in my introduction to this book, I spoke about Abbie, a defendant who was clearly a victim too. Emily is the flip-side of Abbie. A victim can also be a suspect and then a defendant.

Frank was referred to me as a defendant. When I met him at court, his mother explained that Frank was also a witness (alleged victim) in another case that was running concurrently. Initially he had another Intermediary working with him for the latter case, but for the sake of continuity we agreed I would take on both cases. Building a rapport with Frank was so important for both trials, and it was easier for me to understand the issues involved as the cases were also related and involved some of the same people. I attended two trials with Frank. I heard more recently that he needed an Intermediary for another trial, and unfortunately, I was already booked for another case. I have realised after six years that both witnesses and defendants may come around again.

As you may have noticed by this stage of the book, I have described very few gory details of crimes, alleged or otherwise. As an Intermediary, my focus is entirely on communication: ensuring accurate, coherent and clear communication takes place between the two or more people in whichever room, office or court. I do not know how it is for other Intermediaries, but I take very little interest in the crimes. I rarely consider if the defendant is guilty or innocent, I rarely concern myself with whether the witness is telling the truth. I think there are plenty of other people to worry about this – the juries, the barristers and solicitors, the judges and magistrates. I have a singular purpose – maximising communication.

I do not watch crime movies, crime TV programmes or read crime novels. I have never been interested in that sort of fiction, and now that I work with real cases, fictional cases do not appeal at all. I have my fill of the worst side of human nature during my working hours.

Does this mean I am not affected by the details of these crimes? I make extensive use of peer support to ensure I can assimilate my feelings and offload some of the details to those who understand my role. I like to be freely available to a small network of other Intermediaries to hear their experiences and they help me recognise that my experiences are not unique. It is a two-way process, co-counselling in effect, and I value it greatly in this somewhat isolated profession.

The ability to remain non-judgemental and impartial by compartmentalising my work and other parts of my life is crucial. I am not sure if I could have handled this work when I had two young children at home. Being alone and having space to think, while knowing I have secure family and social networks, are vital to me.

Sometimes I am asked to assess a defendant who is in prison, either because he has already been convicted of another crime, or he is on remand. I arrange an appointment, usually as a legal visit or sometimes as a medical visit. I am not a legal professional or a medical person, but there does not seem to be another category. Medical visits can usually be longer and often work better for me. I can spend more than an hour with the prisoner and I can usually get an individual meeting room. It is very difficult to carry out a full communication assessment if we meet in the crowded busy general visiting room.

Each prison's visiting arrangements are different and each one thinks its rules are obvious. Comparing two prisons I have visited, one allowed laptops, the other did not; one allowed the use of an ID card, the other required a passport; one had big lockers provided after going through security, the other expected me to go to a small locker before going through security and know in advance what I could and could not take in. I failed to recognise my Fitbit as a security risk and had to go back around a queue to store it away. I watched a woman in a vest top and poncho be refused entry; luckily a visitors' centre assistant lent her a cardigan, otherwise this woman would have had to go home without seeing her partner. Of course, some of these differences relate to the category of prison, but as a civilian on a one-off visit, I do not know the rules.

I have noticed that the other legal visitors know the routine; it is their local prison and they have probably visited several times. For me, it is another stressful new environment. One visit that stays in my memory was to a very isolated secure unit. I took the train to the nearest station and then waited at the local bus stop. The bus duly arrived and the driver asked me *'single or return?'* I was surprised! I thought a single would mean I was planning to stay at the prison… long term. Later in the day when I tried to leave, I discovered the logic to his question. The return bus only ran once at the end of the afternoon, probably when the shift changed. Leaving the prison after less than a couple of hours, I was stranded outside the building, unsure how to get back. Thankfully, when I approached a prison officer coming off shift, she offered me a lift. She went out of her way home to take me to a convenient train station, for which I was most grateful. Prisons are almost always in very isolated places and travelling by car would probably be a better idea.

Many of my emotions in this work are not related to the criminal details of a case. They are more often frustrations with the legal process and the level of resistance to any new ideas that may challenge deeply held traditions. The inconsistency between courts, previously referred to as postcode lottery, for a travelling Intermediary like myself can be incredibly difficult to not take personally.

I attended a court about a year ago in an area I had worked before. The previous trial had been a very difficult one for me, where I had felt my involvement had not been as effective as I would have liked. The experience preyed on my mind for several weeks and when I realised I had another case in the same court, I was quite depressed by the thought of returning.

I have noticed that when my confidence is shattered by a difficult trial process, it takes some time to pick myself up and re-assert myself. A difficult trial process is not a difficult trial. Difficult trials are when the evidence is emotionally demanding or the information is highly complex and hard to simplify. A difficult trial process is when I find less acceptance of my advisory role and a resistance to adapting to the special needs of a vulnerable witness or defendant.

I was unsure if I would be able to work with the same group of advocates and judge. I tried to remind myself that a judge I had encountered in three different courts, had become progressively more willing to engage with my role and listen to my advice, even if she did not always agree.

A colleague called me a while back to talk about a case where she was to assist a very vulnerable witness attend court for cross-examination. During the trial, we spoke on several occasions and I listened as the issues unfolded. Her experience had many of the hallmarks of the confidence-bashing I had experienced.

Back to my dilemma.

I weighed up the issues if I turned down the case and how I would justify it to myself. Bert, the alleged victim, would either have to manage without an Intermediary or the case might be delayed for several months while another Intermediary was allocated. I started to think it was cowardice that was stopping me going back to that court. Surely, I was stronger than one adverse experience?

I also wondered if one of the reasons the court did not accept my recommendations was that I needed a more assertive approach. Perhaps I needed to report my concerns more often, intervene more often and ask for an adjournment to revisit the ground rules during cross-examination. For those that know Paula Backen, the idea that I was insufficiently assertive might seem strange, but there is a fine balance to be struck during a tense and intense question and answer session.

I persuaded myself to stay with the case. Unfortunately, the police officer in the case was difficult to contact and my attempts to speak with CPS in advance were in vain. On the day before the trial I met Bert at court and the witness service volunteers were particularly accommodating to Bert's needs. The court usher assisted in arranging a familiarisation session, where Bert answered some non-evidential questions in the court behind screens and then via video link. Bert chose to give evidence in court behind screens.

The evening before the start of the trial, defence counsel sent me a list of written questions by email and accepted all my suggested amendments which I sent by return. On arriving at court, both counsel were very positive about my involvement and I started to feel more confident about the forthcoming trial.

At the GRH I sat behind the counsel bench and was not required to go into the witness box. The judge authorised all my recommendations and was very helpful when I mentioned the difficulty of having no police officer available to assist with a 'memory refresh'. He agreed to the psychiatric social worker being present in her place. Particularly reassuring for me, the judge agreed that I could intervene directly to counsel, without having to raise my hand and wait for his Honour's attention.

The judge also agreed to my request that both he and counsel meet Bert briefly in the witness service area before the trial began.

When we started cross examination, it was obvious very quickly that the jury, barristers and judge could not hear Bert clearly; his speech intelligibility was poorer than I had expected. The judge accepted my verbatim repetitions of Bert's responses. On one occasion when the judge started to rephrase at the same time, I apologised for interrupting him, but he replied that he would rather I was the person to speak and rephrase.

Bert left feeling he had been very fairly treated and went home with his support worker. When the trial concluded, the defence counsel sent me an email: "*I thought your input was very valuable.*"

This trial took place in a courtroom adjacent to a courtroom I had attended just a month before, where the vulnerabilities of the witness were, in my opinion, not considered, my recommendations not accepted and the trial had ended when the witness refused to continue to be cross-examined. Same postcode, but a lottery anyway.

In another case referred by police, Francis aged 20 years had not separated from her mother in over a year, often calling out to her mother if she left Francis alone in a room, and only sleeping if her bedroom door was open so she could see into her mother's bedroom. Francis was known to mental health services with a diagnosis of Personality Disorder and Post-Traumatic Stress Disorder. She did not have any Learning Difficulties, and prior to the reported events in her teenage life, had been doing well academically. However, as she had not engaged with the mental health services offered, she was only supported by her mother. She did not leave her home and spoke to no-one other than her mother.

When I initially met Francis, she was in the early stages of reporting her teenage experiences of alleged abuse. Despite several attempts, she refused to continue with a formal evidence interview for criminal proceedings and the case was closed. I heard about her again when the family courts were interested in her evidence in relation to a step-child's custody. She told the social workers that she would only engage if I could assist her. I felt I had a role in finding the best way to enable her to give her evidence. I was however concerned that although she had formed a rapport with me, and may well allow me to assist her in helping the family court, my involvement would cease immediately afterward, and as a result, when she would be at her potentially most vulnerable, she would have no professional support to fall back on. As it happened, despite my involvement in a very productive GRH and lots of well-laid plans, Francis refused at the last hurdle to participate as a witness.

This lack of continued involvement is a concern when Intermediaries work with psychologically damaged individuals. With witnesses, our involvement ceases as soon as the witness is stood down by the court. This may well be a very vulnerable time for the witness, after the experience of cross-examination. In most cases, there are police officers available with whom the witness has formed a long-term relationship and who can see them again over the coming weeks. Francis was, I hope, a rare exception.

For defendants, the involvement of the Intermediary may conclude at various points in the process. In some trials where I have been present from the start, the judge only authorises my presence until the end of the defendant's evidence. The defendant then returns to the dock alone for the rest of the proceedings. There may be other defence witnesses and some statements to be read, but it is often just the closing speeches of the barristers and summing up by the judge. I appreciate this may seem a less important phase for the defendant, but I often feel uneasy leaving at this stage. If the funding has been authorised until the end of the day, I ask the judge if I can stay for that time. This is not always granted.

On other occasions, the judge sends me away when the jury retires to decide their verdict. This may be a decision based on costs, as the time a jury is out is unpredictable, and in effect I have very little to do until we are recalled for the verdict.

These circumstances raise the issue of whether an Intermediary is there because the defendant is vulnerable or whether her presence is solely to maximise understanding and communication. In effect, the defendant's vulnerability is his communication disability and his poor communication skills are his vulnerability.

Harriet was charged and required to attend court for a four-day trial at a crown court. She was not sure what would happen but she did know that she was already having panic attacks whenever she thought about it. I sat beside her for four days, helping her to understand and talk with her barrister. She was accused of taking money from an elderly woman, and throughout the trial I did not try to guess at the verdict or concern myself with whether she committed this crime. At one point, there was a chance that I would be sent away, as the judge was not convinced of Harriet's vulnerability and limited communication skills. While we waited for the judge to decide, Harriet told me that if I was sent away, she would run out of court and not return unless she was arrested. Eventually the judge did permit my involvement. The trial continued for four days. The jury acquitted Harriet. We had discussed possible outcomes of the trial on several occasions with the barrister. However, while we waited for the verdict, Harriet asked me again what the judge would do to her if she was found '*not guilty*'. She was genuinely surprised to hear she would be able to go home and get on with her life.

I think Harriet had been punished in advance of the verdict: panic attacks and stress for over a year and then four days in a locked glassed dock. Is there more the legal system can do to mitigate against this? I do not have an answer but I think this situation for particularly vulnerable and traumatised people is worthy of attention. For witnesses, this situation occurs when an acquittal leaves the victim feeling that perhaps she should not have gone to the police in the first place. This is outside the role of the Intermediary, but as part of the legal system I am aware of these tensions.

In so many of the cases referred to me, both defendant and alleged victim, the charges are related to sexual crimes. In May 2017, the BBC screened the dramatisation of the Rochdale case of sexual grooming and abuse of teenage girls (9). The three-hour long programme dealt with many aspects of the way vulnerable young people, one of whom had some additional special needs, were viewed by the police. The health worker argued with the police that these girls were not prostitutes, as any girl under 16 could not make that choice to consent to sex. I was surprised that Intermediaries were not involved in either the videoed police interviews of the youngest girl or in the witnesses' preparation for court. An Intermediary would probably have advised against the girls watching their videos with the court, as I have described for Emily above. The level and length of cross-examination was surprising also. Legislation recommends that judges limit the length of questioning and suggests that one barrister asks most of the questions in a case of multiple defendants. In the programme, it seemed that questioning spanned several days for each witness and involved many barristers challenging the witnesses. There must be a better way for victims to help the court without being re-traumatised and I would have hoped that more than 10 years after the introduction of Intermediaries, the justice system might have got the message in this case. Of course, I do not know the full details, only those revealed in the dramatisation.

"I haven't written my questions down in 30 years!"

The Intermediary impacts on the traditions and practices of the legal system. She is most effective when able to challenge established beliefs and customs, using research and experience from disciplines with which lawyers are unfamiliar. This can result in a more flexible approach to vulnerable people.

The courts have been directed to take every reasonable step to facilitate participation of both witnesses and defendants. As I have mentioned there is a wide-ranging response to this direction. The response depends on an understanding of vulnerability, and the openness to change among court staff, legal advocates, police and judges. In this chapter, I detail some examples of effective changes that I have experienced during my work.

Establishing my neutrality and duty to the court can be fundamental in achieving change. I have observed many an alarmed expression when I have asked to see cross-examination questions in advance. There is an assumption that I will automatically share my knowledge with the witness and thus prepare him inappropriately. I recently attended a Court of Appeal hearing to give evidence myself of my experience of acting as an Intermediary, and one of the judges looked quite surprised that this practice of reviewing questions was widespread, although it is commended as good practice by the Court of Appeal itself. On some occasions, both defence and prosecution advocates have wanted to be present during these discussions, concerned to ensure 'fair play'.

When I asked one defence barrister if I could discuss his planned questions for cross-examination of Ella, his response was not unique: "*I haven't written my questions down in 30 years and I don't intend to now!*" The idea of presenting written questions, in his opinion, suggested that he was new to the Bar, inexperienced and unlikely to be able to think on his feet when a witness gave an unexpected answer. (In fact, preparation of written questions for review is the foundation of the Inns of Court College of Advocacy current training on questioning vulnerable persons.) I explained to him that discussing questions in advance would not preclude spontaneity in his cross-examination. By discussing the questions in advance, he would most probably become used to the ground rules to make his questions more effective. If not, I could intervene and assist in real-time.

I find myself often having to remind the court that my interest is not particularly in the line of questioning, but rather in the manner in which the question is asked, and the ability of the witness to give a coherent and accurate answer. I am interested in the vocabulary used, the grammatical structure of the question, and often the order of questions. Here are some examples.

'On the occasion of the incident on 15th September 2015, were you at the address or were you staying with a friend?" could be replaced with:

"That Thursday, were you at Pete's house?"

"Has this happened on more than one occasion?" could be replaced with:

"How many times did you stay at Pete's house?"

When counsel and judges are asked to keep their questions simple, they sometimes respond by saying the complex word, followed by the simple one eg *'when you administered, or you gave her the medicine…'.* They may also ask the question in three different ways, in the hope that one of them will be understood. So that *'Did you want to go there?'* becomes *'when you were asked to go to the party, what did you think…were you interested in attending…you didn't want to go, did you?'* By which stage the witness is not sure which question to answer, whether the last part was a negative or a positive, or whether there was more than one part to answer.

Judges have been directed for many years now to ensure questions focus on the matters at issue and to impose restrictions on asking about specific topics. For example, if defence counsel wants to ask about previous bad character of a witness, there will be a legal argument and a decision made about whether the question can be posed. Similarly, decisions are made about the admissibility of previous sexual activity or events unrelated to the case.

There are occasionally exceptions to this. For example, if I have found in my assessment that the witness struggles with concepts of time, I will advise the court on the level of accuracy that is likely to be achieved by posing a question about time or timing of events, or suggest the use of a visual aid to improve accuracy. Sometimes this is just in the form of a series of coloured post-its positioned on a large piece of paper, or a A4 sheet split into a calendar sheet, with the relevant events handwritten into each day.

If distance is important, I may recommend a measure that will be understood by the witness. Finn had an IQ of 61 and was assessed to have a limited concept of distance. However, as a manual labourer, he was used to identifying distance in terms of the number of houses along the road. When the barrister asked, *"How far away was the man?"* I rephrased this as *"How many houses away were you?"*

I also need to check the order of questions; if a witness is suggestible, then presenting a series of four questions to which she will answer *'yes'*, may result in her answering positively to the fifth vital question, when she has previously denied this matter.

A police officer who had interviewed a vulnerable alleged victim without an Intermediary, showed me the ABE recording and asked me for some advice on how she could have improved her questioning. The case was not proceeding to trial - a decision made by her chief inspector - and I was not involved in the case. Here are some examples of the changes I suggested to her when I reviewed the video-recording:

You said:	Try this instead:
In relation to him moving	*When he moved…*
Since the incident…	*After it happened… or since it*

	happened...
The times you have seen him...	*When you saw him...*
Can you tell me what he said?	*What did John say?*
Has that happened on more than one occasion?	*How many times did that happen?*
So, people have been present...	*Were other people there?*
Was any clothing removed?	*Did you take any clothes off? Did he take your clothes off?*

Many of these suggestions were just about shortening the sentence or using simpler vocabulary. In the last example, I turned a passive tense into an active tense which is generally easier to understand. On one occasion, I suggested putting the person's name, rather than a pronoun, as it might not have been clear who the officer was asking about. I may advise on the avoidance of non-literal or figurative language eg 'let's cut to the chase' or 'my hands are tied'. Officers and court advocates are well practised in using terms like 'incident', 'occasion' and 'in relation to', when these are not common parlance. The term 'address' in court does not relate to the number of the house, road and postcode; it means the house or flat, and this can be very confusing for someone with limited understanding.

These examples are not exhaustive but represent a small proportion of the advice an Intermediary may recommend.

My adaptations to the court process do not rest at the question formats for evidence. I emphasise this, as I have found some courts reduce the involvement of an Intermediary to a discussion about questions. My interest is in the whole communicative environment and how this can be adapted to achieve the best communication from and with a vulnerable person.

One major area of adaptation is the physical environment: is it better for the witness to give evidence in the courtroom, from a witness box, or behind a screen so that the witness cannot see the defendant or the public gallery? Sometimes giving evidence in a large courtroom, being looked at by so many people, will cause the witness such distress as to make the evidence less coherent and accurate. A live link room would be better option.

I have mentioned in a previous chapter that if a live link room is used, the defendant can see the witness on the TV monitor and this may cause some concern for the witness. There is another special measure which can be used to good effect: where screens are used to prevent the defendant from seeing the TV monitor. Intermediaries and courts have found imaginative ways to do this screening: using newspaper stuck to the dock glass to obscure the view; moving the defendant to the press gallery and adding a screen; or turning off the main TV monitors and using small desk monitors for the jury and advocates, without providing one for the defendant.

Other aspects of the environment that need to be considered include: the removal of wigs and gowns by the barristers (and judge); allowing a witness to sit rather than stand in the witness box; giving the witness an 'I need a break' card to point to. Often,

I see the witness and their family look surprised that such adaptations are possible. Many are influenced by watching TV dramas, and assume this is reality.

Once the environment is adapted, I then think about how the vulnerable person will get to that environment. I make recommendations about timings. When Thomas was required to give evidence as an alleged victim, I considered his sleep pattern (rarely waking before 11am) and recommended that he give evidence in the afternoon court session. For some defendants, I advise the court that if the trial does not reach his evidence until after 3pm, it may be better to adjourn until morning. He is likely to be fatigued from the day's proceedings, and less likely to provide his best evidence. For witnesses and defendants, other factors which will impact on this decision include the expected length of questioning, how long the witness has been waiting, and whether it will be difficult to ask her to wait over a weekend to complete the process. The judge of course is ultimately responsible and has the whole picture, but the Intermediary is focussed on these specific matters and can provide valuable advice.

Ryan was asked to attend court for cross-examination in advance of the trial, using the new 'section 28' pre-recording special measure for witnesses. He struggled to go to sleep before 4am and I had originally requested an afternoon attendance. Unfortunately, I was told that this particular court did all 'section 28s' at 9.30am to avoid clashing with other trial listings. So, in an effort to provide this witness with the advantage of a pre-recorded cross-examination, he was disadvantaged in having to attend in a drowsy state.

For witnesses attending during a trial, there is a well-rehearsed pathway in most courts for allowing access to a secure area of the court building without the chance of meeting the defendant or his supporters around the entrance. This is arranged with the witness service volunteers, and for the most part is highly effective. The witness service provides a calming, reassuring environment. If the witness is using screens to avoid being seen by the defendant, getting into the courtroom can be more problematic. Access into court is less consistent across the country: in some courts, there is an alternative route into the courtroom via long corridors and often the judge's entrance. Alternatively, the defendant waits in a separate room (sometimes behind the dock) until the witness is in place behind screens.

Defendants are expected to wait in the general waiting area of the court building until their trial and in the breaks. For many vulnerable defendants, I recommend that a small meeting room on the corridor is set aside to give the defendant a quiet place. When the time comes to give evidence, getting to the witness box from the dock with the jury, barristers, judge and press observing can be a very stressful few steps. I often recommend that the defendant takes up position in the box in an almost empty courtroom before the judge and jury arrive, allowing him a few moments to settle. For some defendants, particularly with mental health issues or Autistic Spectrum Disorder, this can be an important adaptation.

As mentioned before, not all witnesses go into the courtroom. Link rooms within court are a well-used option, as is the increasing use of remote links, from police stations, witness's homes, care homes or police interview suites. These ensure witnesses do not encounter the defendant or the defendant's family, and keep the witness away from the imposing court building. In more rural parts of the country, it can also help avoid the lengthy journeys to court.

Once in the most conducive environment we can create, the witness may be more able to communicate when sitting on the floor, writing her responses, or whispering them to the Intermediary who speaks them to the court. I have assisted defendants whose speech is so unclear, that I have had to repeat almost every response (other than yes or no) to achieve intelligibility for the court. Those Intermediaries who work with other client groups eg hearing impaired and small children have many other strategies. I experienced one case where the magistrates could not understand the strongly accented English of the defendant and I was permitted to repeat his answers for the court.

The speed of delivery of questions may also be important. The arraignment and other instructions by the court clerk, or the caution read by the police to a suspect, are usually delivered quickly and in an automated fashion. This can make it difficult for the person with poor auditory processing skills. I often ask for advocates to slow down their questions and give plenty of time for a response. Jules could respond to simple questions, but he needed at least 3-4 seconds to process the question and access the words to respond. The District Judge did not allow me to address her fully in a GRH in Jules' case, and although I made clear recommendations in my report that Jules needed a long pause before responding, the District Judge intervened to rephrase the question during the first silence. I intervened on the second example of this, and addressed the District Judge directly, asking for time for Jules to think and respond. The District Judge agreed. Jules was then able to continue to be cross-examined without any further interventions.

With the defendant, there may be some very simple environmental changes which have a considerable impact on his effective participation in the whole trial. For example, when Kyle and I arrived in a courtroom with a small dock containing two rows of two seats, for a trial of three co-defendants, I recognised that it would be very difficult to accommodate everyone's needs. One of the co-defendants had binaural hearing loss and needed to sit forward to lip read and listen to the court. I needed to whisper explanations to Kyle and if we sat behind them, we might have affected the other defendants' ability to focus.

I addressed the judge on this matter, and the clerk successfully located a courtroom with a bigger dock to which we transferred before starting the trial. The new dock had eight seats in one row. I sat at one end with Kyle beside me and the other two defendants sat a few seats away from us. Interestingly, although generally I dislike fully glassed docks, in this case the powerful speakers installed in the dock were helpful to us all.

Courts usually sit for around three hours in the morning and two and half hours in the afternoon. Most judges allow for at least one break in the morning, but for the jury there may be several breaks when the court addresses legal matters that need to be heard without them. Sitting in a dock, listening and not contributing on matters that are highly emotive, can be a struggle for even a non-vulnerable person. For the vulnerable defendant, with a limited concentration span, heightened anxiety and less than full understanding of the proceedings, it is quite a feat. However, there are sections of a trial process that require more focus than others.

When I assessed Leo, I could see the impact of timing and breaks on his concentration. After around 20 minutes of various assessment tasks, there was a clear deterioration in his performance and he needed a break. After a quick cigarette and a coffee, he returned refreshed. I advised the court that when he gave evidence he would need breaks every 20 minutes. However, when we sat in the dock, and the barristers were debating a legal argument, or the judge was summing up the case, Leo could sit for over an hour without a break. During this time, he did not need to respond or understand any new evidence. He benefitted from the use of tangle toys and some doodling on an iPad with me, and the court could complete its business without adjournment. I explained the judge's decision at the end of the legal argument, during a subsequent break.

I have mentioned previously that many of the defendants referred to an Intermediary are in the dock with co-defendants. Some of these trials can be many weeks long with only a small part of the trial related to the vulnerable person I am assisting. I recall a particularly extreme case of this, when Albert was tried along with eight other defendants in a case listed to last for three months. The charges were multiple and complex, but Albert was only named on one count. He was medically unwell and had some Learning Difficulties, and with the help of his counsel, I suggested to court that he be excused for some trial days. Sometimes it is possible to have a separate trial for a defendant like Albert, called 'severing the case', but his barrister explained the legal aspects which meant this would not be possible.

As I have illustrated, the remit of an Intermediary is greater than just the questions to be asked during cross-examination. It encompasses anything which may affect communication and understanding in their widest sense. Each case is a new set of circumstances and demands creativity. I find each trial unique and challenging, suggesting there is not a simple checklist which can be provided to the court which would cover every eventuality. In recent years, The Advocate's Gateway has developed a set of 'Toolkits' which cover the main vulnerabilities and advice to advocates on best practice. These are by their very nature generic, and must be recognised as such; but they offer a useful starting point from which the court can build an appropriate approach for the individual with the assistance of the Intermediary.

Of course, I rarely get to see a court hearing when I am not involved. I do wonder about those cases where no legal professional has identified the vulnerability of a defendant or witness.

However, one day I was waiting for the next case, and observed the last five minutes of a magistrates' trial. A young man in the dock was asked to stand while the magistrate read out the verdict. At the end of a long narrative, the magistrate said '...*so you are acquitted*'. The family sat quietly, the defendant stayed standing. The magistrates picked up their papers and left the court. Clearly the young man had not understood. The security officer piped up '*You are being let off!*', and the family cheered and everyone left the court.

In comparison, at the end of a case in the magistrates' court, where I had advised the bench on communication strategies, the magistrate addressed the defendant Archie directly and said: "*I am going to start by telling you our decision. We have decided you are **not guilty**. (Pause) Now I have to say the reasons and it will take a few minutes. When I have finished you can go home.*"

"Communication means being able to speak"

I will now address the various abilities and disabilities that the legal system encounters, and some of the terminology used to describe communication issues which confuse the way vulnerability is viewed. I need to go back to my original career to put this in context.

When the Speech Therapy profession decided to change its title during the 1990's, they nationally canvassed the practitioners and a decision was made to change to Speech and Language Therapy. At the time, I recall my disappointment that this change would not assist the public in understanding the wide range of our professional skills. If we ask the public for the meaning of 'speech' and 'language' the distinction is neither clear nor encompasses the multiple areas of communication we address. In simple terms, speech concerns the production of words by the tongue lips, larynx. Language is about the understanding, storing and processing of words in our brains, and the subsequent accessing and combining of words, to form a communication by speech / signing / writing or otherwise. There are many other aspects to communication and it not the remit of this book to provide a full description. It is important to recognise the manner, context, and non-verbal aspects of communication in its widest sense.

Disordered or impaired communication is even more complicated.

The Intermediary is concerned about the full range of communication, verbal and non-verbal. However, unlike the

Speech and Language Therapist, the Intermediary is not looking to provide therapy or improve the communication skills of the client, rather to maximise his communication in the specific environment of the interview suite or court room.

Mindy managed to get by in life as she was part of a very close family unit. Her husband cooked and shopped, her parents helped her with getting to her cleaning job which she had kept for years and knew the routines. She was functionally illiterate so any reading of letters and filling forms was left to the family. Her teenage daughter was both very academic and mature for her years, and organised many aspects of their life. First impressions would conclude that Mindy was a well-dressed, very presentable able person. She spoke clearly if infrequently. Quite quickly, however, it became clear that she deferred to her partner in all matters. Her facial expression was of very limited range and she looked quite blank when addressed directly. Only on full assessment was it clear that despite 'getting by' she had extremely poor auditory language skills, perhaps at a level expected from a six-year-old child. When she was arrested she refused a solicitor as, in her view, *'I have not done anything wrong'*. The police did not recognise that Mindy had any disabilities. When she spoke, she spoke clearly. As a result, there was no appropriate adult, nor legal representative at her police interview.

Interestingly, when a witness manages to provide video evidence in a police interview, without an Intermediary, the court may challenge the recommendations of an Intermediary to assist at court for cross-examination. The communication environment and demands of a courtroom are considerably greater than in the one-to-one sofa chat of a police interview suite, and when the Intermediary explains this, many judges accept the need for assistance in court.

When Mindy's case was to be heard in court, the judge had no qualms about granting an Intermediary, as he saw the complexity of court language and process to be more than Mindy could manage. The judge was presented with expert witness reports from psychologists and a speech & language therapist that confirmed Mindy's struggle to comprehend language, both in written and oral forms. This did not mean she could not speak. The judge also listened to the audio recording of the police interview and from Mindy's responses, determined that what she admitted to in interview (without any assistance during complex questioning) should be presented to the jury at trial. I do not think the judge entirely *'got it'*.

When someone can speak, it does not mean they understand at the level expected of their age. When Mindy was left to speak uninterrupted, she could give a simple narrative of the events as she recalled them. However, as soon as a question was asked of her, she was required to use her auditory verbal processing skills, and then became uncertain how to answer. If the vocabulary was kept simple and the question short, Mindy was a competent communicator for the purposes of the court.

A diagnosis of Dyslexia is not always limited to difficulties with reading and writing. In Neil's case, he attended a police station for a suspect interview, but as he only said he was Dyslexic, it was concluded he would be able to cope with an audio-recorded interview without an appropriate adult.

An appropriate adult is a parent, guardian or social worker; or if no person matching this is available, any responsible person over 18, in England and Wales, who will safeguard the interests of a child or vulnerable adult. They can be present for a range of police processes, including interviews, intimate searches and identification procedures, but are not used in the court system. Just as an aside, I arrived at a South London train station one morning, in search of the local police station. When I asked two young men, they said they would show me the way and then asked, *'Are you an appropriate adult?'* Something in the way I spoke or looked had made them think I was a supporter or enabler, and not a police officer, complainant or criminal!

When I assessed Neil, he had significant word retrieval difficulties and issues with sequencing accurately. These impacted on his ability to describe his version of events. However, the judge in Neil's case said there were many successful people in our society who were dyslexic, so we could not presume that such a diagnosis should alert police to the vulnerability of a suspect. There is an issue to address here – how can a police officer or a solicitor recognise a communication need especially when it is a hidden vulnerability? Are there some simple questions to be asked which would alert the professional to request further information? Indeed, there are. Asking the suspect or the alleged victim about their experience of school, whether they live independently, and whether they need help with their money, would be a great start. Some police forces have started to use a simple checklist, although of course there will always be concerns about the false negatives / positives of any screening test.

I have also noticed another pattern among both witnesses and defendants when I meet them for an assessment. They are happy to admit to being dyslexic, but this is often a cover for further Learning Difficulties which, perhaps in their mind, could define them as stupid. Dyslexia has become an acceptable label for all social classes. However, it may be that it covers up a more general low cognitive functioning, or other specific learning disabilities.

This is understandable in a world that still defines intelligence in a very narrow manner. Accepting that there are other types of intelligences, aside from the traditional dependence on specific IQ score, would perhaps help improve our appreciation of the complex range of human abilities. A man who cannot read or write may well be a fantastic painter and decorator, with superior skills in colour matching, and be far better at organising his daily responsibilities than a man with a PhD in Chemical Engineering. For example, Ken was illiterate and could not be depended upon to remember the two items he was asked to shop for, but he was an amazing long-distance runner because he could focus his mind on the physical task. As his proud daughter told me, *"My dad is the best in the world at slicing garlic!"* I am sure that modern society is starting to appreciate this approach to multiple intelligences, but the legal system seems a long way behind.

An understanding of the fluctuating nature of mental health also seems to pass the courts by. Living with a mental health condition invariably involves managing the ups and downs. Indeed, from day to day, and sometimes even by the hour. Josephine, a 16-year-old witness I met for an assessment in a secure psychiatric unit, was initially struggling to enter an unfamiliar room and could not stay to chat for more than ten minutes. A year later, when we met at court for a pre-trial familiarisation visit, she was living with her parents and, apart from the self-harming scars on her arms, she seemed emotionally able to cope with the unfamiliar environment. She stated bravely that she would be giving evidence in open court without any screens. Two weeks later at court, she had a panic attack before leaving home, and despite medication on arrival, she chose to use a link room away from the court. Explaining this to the judge and barristers was hard work: the change in recommendations did not meet with approval. One barrister remonstrated that I should not be permitted "*to change my recommendations from those in the written report*".

Mel came to court full of confidence. She had the support of a police officer on her journey and did not view the court as anything more than a new exciting experience. She was in her fifties, had Learning Difficulties and lived successfully in a supported group home. Although she had reported being raped by a staff member, she did not seem overly anxious when talking about the incident. She certainly had an optimistic view of the world and did her best to keep both the officer and I in good spirits with her humour. She spoke freely about her previous sexual experiences, was a little disinhibited and unaware of social norms. She struggled to retain the plans for attending court, and was highly dependent on the staff and police officer to alert her to times and arrangements. She had been interviewed for her evidence without an Intermediary involved. The police officer thought that as Mel spoke so fluently, albeit in simple vocabulary, she would be able to describe her experience. When the case proceeded to trial, the CPS wanted an Intermediary involved. Mel had not been seen by either psychologists or psychiatrists for years, but there was sufficient Community Mental Health records to confirm her vulnerability and the judge agreed to my appointment to assist Mel. We agreed that a large courtroom would be too intimidating, but she was at ease with the link room arrangement.

The case was essentially a trial of two matters: whether the staff member had had sex with Mel; and whether she had consented to the sex act. The staff member pleaded guilty to the first issue and as she was in his care, this was a criminal offence. Mel repeatedly said to the officer *'I didn't want him to do it'*. That seemed very clear. However, when we got to cross-examination, Mel told the court *'I did want sex, but I didn't like the way he did it''*. He was convicted of the first count and acquitted of the second count.

A friend, who has worked in the social housing sector for many years, commented to me recently: *"public services are just not recognising those vulnerable people who are borderline — not living in care homes or hospitals, who are supposed to attend mainstream schools — who cannot cope with the complex systems of the 21st Century."* There are times when I wonder how anyone without a good grade GCSE English copes with the forms, processes and rules of our technical society. Just booking a train ticket, finding the platform and a seat is more than most of my clients can handle. Many legal professionals have little insight into these difficulties.

"Can we get three Intermediaries into one trial?"

Everyone who works in a specialist field is in a bubble of sorts. I met a probation officer years ago who specialised in working with sexual abuse criminals. She had two young sons and she struggled to trust anyone other than her husband to look after them. She had developed the skewed impression that no man could be trusted to keep his hands off her children. I had some sympathy for her: she spent so much time working with paedophiles, that she had lost her ability to recognise the bigger picture.

Widely accepted research on young offenders shows that around 60% have speech, language and communication needs (10), and across all ages, disability is strongly over-represented in the justice system. I have noticed however, in those cases where I work with a vulnerable alleged victim, the perpetrator is rarely a vulnerable person.

There are exceptions. In a recent trial, the alleged crime took place within a close family network. Julie was accused of systematic theft over several years from the bank account of her grandfather Howard. Julie's partner and father were asked to give evidence as part of her defence. It did not take long for Julie's solicitor to recognise that all the family had Learning Difficulties of varying degrees. When the police interviewed Howard, it was clear he struggled to express himself and understand the questions. To add to these complications, the events took place more than four years before Howard reported them to the police.

A trial was listed to commence in June. An Intermediary was arranged for Julie and another for Howard. On the first day of the trial, the defence barrister addressed the judge about his concerns regarding Julie's partner and father's ability to give evidence without the assistance of an Intermediary. The case was adjourned for several months, whilst a third Intermediary was found for these two defence witnesses. The National Crime Agency (NCA) manages a matching system for the prosecution witnesses, and due to increased demand year on year, does not routinely offer this service to defence witnesses. However, the judge made a special request to the NCA and I was duly appointed.

In December, I arrived at court on the first day of trial, only to find that the court had not re-booked Julie's Intermediary. So, the court again had two out of three Intermediaries and was at pains to work out how to proceed. I was asked if I could assist Julie in the dock. I explained that to do so, I would have to read her Intermediary report, spend some time with her to ensure I agreed with the findings, and then the two defence witnesses would not have an Intermediary and the court would be back to where they were in June.

I mention this case, not to allocate blame, but to indicate again the complexity of arranging a trial. While I waited in the court building for the judge to decide on the best next steps, I revisited my conclusions on the defence witnesses' communication skills. They were sitting beside me. The barrister asked for Julie's phone number, as she had changed it without informing anyone involved in her case. I watched as Julie, her partner and her father inspected all their phones for several minutes, trying to work out how to get Julie's number. Jointly, they could not complete this basic task. Their literacy and problem-solving skills were too limited. They clearly could not cope with the complexity of a court trial without assistance.

When I work in a case where more than one person has special needs, I sometimes feel as if I have entered a 'zone' which has a different set of norms. Julie's family manage most of the time with minimal interventions from community support services. They live in their limited world, with perhaps less of the stresses of daily life you and I experience, such as getting to work on time, managing bank accounts and planning for our future. Perhaps they live more in the moment that I do. I am not suggesting here that they are better off, lucky or happier, or indeed the reverse. I just find it can be a different world, and I endeavour not to make assumptions about my client's priorities. When it was time to leave, the barrister apologised to everyone about the repeated postponement of the trial. Julie's father looked confused: he replied that he had enjoyed a great day out, sitting in the waiting area of the court and was off to have a well-earned cup of tea!

****

Every case has such differing demands. Having assessed the client and recommended how the trial would be best adapted to his vulnerability, I then wait to see what the judge, barrister and courtroom will be willing and able to accommodate.

Sometimes a vulnerable witness is referred with major concerns about his ability to participate at all in giving evidence. I have a professional duty to consider my own competencies in these situations. For example, I have very little clinical experience with people with severe Learning Difficulties or with non-verbal / signing communicators, so I do not accept such referrals.

Referral forms for witnesses are filled out by police officers and CPS staff. There is often a call with the Registered Intermediary community for referrers to be more accurate about the vulnerability of each witness. Sometimes the level of impairment or diagnosis is not clear from the referral form. This can go two ways. Angela was referred with *'severe Learning Difficulties'* and the National Crime Agency struggled for weeks to match her with a suitably specialised Registered Intermediary. When I noticed the extensive delay, I offered to call the referring officer and find out some more details. Angela was described to me as having the *'reading age of an 8-year-old'*. In my books, this is not 'severe' and I was therefore able to assist with the case, as it was within the scope of my competencies. There may have been other Intermediaries who could have been matched sooner, if the level of impairment had been more accurate.

On the other hand, a witness Donald was referred with mental health issues. From the referral, this seemed well within my competencies. Donald lived in his own home with 24-hour specialist care. I spoke with his key worker who had helped him move from a secure hospital, three years beforehand. Donald was described as having Autistic Spectrum Disorder with aggressive behaviours and was at high risk of self-harm. He had some experience of being arrested by police and was very wary of their presence in his home. The key worker sat with us in a neighbouring house and completed a long risk assessment document, while reinforcing his opinion that it would be very hard to engage with Donald. I decided to avoid any protracted direct assessment session with him and use the information from the key worker to inform my advice to the interviewing officer. I reasoned that his key worker knew Donald far better than I did and would know the best way to communicate. And indeed, I gained quite a lot of information from him; that I should lower my eyes and avoid eye contact, sit in open posture with my hands together and be aware but ignore Donald's sexualised inappropriate comments.

When we met Donald, I noted some other aspects of his communication and included these observations in my recommendations to the police officer who would be interviewing him. I recommended using short simple responses with very little narrative or preamble; not asking about timing as Donald had very little grasp of the concept of time; and not to use idiomatic speech eg *'bear with me'* as he would take these phrases literally. I was concerned about Donald being asked to talk about his traumatic experiences in the normally safe surroundings of his living room. Recounting these experiences could become attached to the environment and he might relive these memories whenever he was in the room. We agreed to meet the following day in an interview suite away from his home where he could leave the memories behind him and maintain the safety of his home environment. My recommendations had been formed more from observations and discussions with others, rather than more structured assessments, but they seemed appropriate.

Sometimes a defendant has been found fit to plead, but on assessment by an Intermediary, his level of communication is so poor as to make it unlikely he could participate effectively in his trial. One Monday lunchtime, I was called by a judge from a crown court. He was at the beginning of a five-day trial and it was being held up as the judge was concerned about the Evelyn's ability to participate. He asked if I could assist and I responded that I only had one day available, the following day. An Intermediary assessment had been carried out and a report filed, but the assessing Intermediary was not available. The judge explained that Evelyn had been excused from giving evidence but he wanted to be sure she understood what was going on and could instruct her counsel. The judge was most persuasive and I agreed to attend, on the basis that I could see all the papers overnight including the Intermediary report and spend some time early morning getting to know Evelyn to review her needs.

Evelyn was in her mid-twenties, with an IQ of 53 and very limited immediate recall of information. She had performed very poorly on tests of understanding grammatical structures and her vocabulary had been assessed as approximating to a child at infant school. She suffered from Epilepsy, not fully controlled by medication, and her partner was her full-time carer.

When we met, Evelyn had been in court the previous day but did not know what the jury was or their role in the trial. I explained this to her and within an hour asked her to explain this to her barrister in my presence, but she had not retained the information. The barrister was most grateful for my involvement and I noted that although he tried to simplify his explanations, many concepts were complex. I used single word reminder cards and pictorial lists. At a short GRH, the judge agreed to my suggestions on how my presence in the dock would be explained to the jury. When Evelyn told me she "*fiddled with her hands a lot*", I gave her a large ball of Blue Tack and tangle toys to distract her. Toward the end of the day I recognised that Evelyn had learned to look at me when she was unsure. In discussion with her barrister, I assisted her understanding of the implications of not giving evidence in her trial.

I was surprised to leave the court that day feeling that my input had been effective and worthwhile. I had been so doubtful that one day out of five, and not for evidence, would be beneficial. The judge commended me in front of the jury, and Evelyn was clearly relieved to have someone to turn to for explanations. I was certain that she had participated more fully with my assistance. So, the part-trial involvement of an Intermediary can be of some benefit in a minority of situations, although interestingly this was for the trial process and not for her to give her own evidence.

In another case, a solicitor contacted me at the end of the first week of a six-week trial. Fran was in court alongside her sister, charged with murder. Fran had been diagnosed with early onset Dementia, but had been deemed fit to plead by two out of three psychiatrists. Currently, a judge makes the final decision on fitness to plead after hearing from at least two medical assessments, and this is not something an Intermediary can comment on. In 2016, The Law Commission reported that the Fitness to Plead test was outdated, inadequate and inconsistent, and made a series of recommendations for improving the test.

The solicitor asked me if I could assess Fran urgently and make recommendations to the court. I agreed, quite madly I know, to see her on the Saturday afternoon and produce a report for start of proceedings in court on Monday. I say, 'quite madly' as I am sure some of my colleagues and most of my friends would think I am both a workaholic and unable to manage my work-life balance. They are probably right, but then we can't all be perfect! I justified it to myself that Fran was in a very difficult situation and time was short. I had no opinion about Fran's guilt or innocence. I just wanted to see if there was a way to help her participate effectively in a trial with potentially grave consequences for her and her co-defendant.

My assessment showed that Fran could not hold onto new information. For example, I told her the town I had travelled from and we discussed whether she had visited there. When I asked her two minutes later, she was unable to recall the name of the town. I introduced the use of three or four post-its with single words on such as types of foods she might want to eat or colours she preferred. She could pick up the post-it she had chosen and keep it beside her, as a memory aid. But these were only useful when I could offer her the words in advance – she was unable to name colours or items independently. This strategy would not help in the complexity of the trial. She did not indicate when she had not understood a complicated word and often guessed at the right answer for even simple questions. Even with a diagram, she could not describe the relationships in her family or name the people. She explained that she struggled to leave home alone, and had become lost on her way to our meeting despite having lived in the area all her life. I advised the court that an Intermediary was unlikely to bring her to a full participative level. Intermediaries clearly are not magicians! This is a grey area where a defendant is deemed fit to plead, but even an Intermediary cannot assist them to properly take part in their trial.

For a vulnerable witness, the level of capacity may be highly significant in determining whether a crime can proceed to court. Ginny was in her thirties with Learning Difficulties, assessed as having an IQ of 55 and was living alone with social services support. She reported that she had been sexually abused. She was open about her alcohol dependency. When assessed, she had very low auditory comprehension and whilst being able to narrate simple explanations, she often steered conversations toward topics she felt more confident with. She became angry and quite aggressive when she did not understand or feared she was losing control of the situation.

Following a psychiatric report that deemed her not to have capacity to consent to sex, the CPS planned to proceed with the case and asked for an Intermediary to assist at court. Ginny was very anxious in all strange or novel environments and did not want to go to court. She needed to be transported by support staff to any location and was not permitted alcohol in the car. I decided that she would not cope well with questioning by a lawyer over a video link and would require questions to be asked very simply.

The defendant in Ginny's case had admitted to the sexual acts but said it had been consensual. However, as she lacked capacity, could she be cross-examined? This assessment is beyond the remit of an Intermediary. When Ginny refused to go to court, the case was dropped by the CPS as they said there was no case to answer.

I recall another case where the defendant admitted to having sex with Bonny, who had not been assessed for capacity. The defendant admitted to sex, but stated that the act had been consensual. The judge ruled that defence could therefore only ask Bonny one question – *"Did you want this to happen?"* This seemed the fairest solution. Bonny explained emphatically that she did not know this man and certainly had not wanted any physical contact with   him.

"I can't tell the time but I know which month it is"

The defendant Jill had been found guilty in a magistrates' court and given a custodial sentence. Jill's parents approached a different firm of solicitors and launched an appeal on her conviction. Such appeals are heard in the crown court by a judge and two magistrates. She had not had the assistance of an Intermediary at her first trial.

Jill had attended special schools throughout her education, having been diagnosed with Learning Difficulties. She had continued to live with her parents as an adult, now aged 35, as she needed both their practical and emotional support. She was in receipt of disability benefits and could not read or write.

I met Jill in prison for an assessment appointment. She was accompanied by a prison listener (another inmate who has been trained to support peers with mental health issues) who explained that Jill was not coping with prison life, tending to cry or laugh several times a day, often inappropriately. Jill told me that without this prison listener, who was sharing her cell, she would not know how to get by each day and she had daily thoughts of suicide.

My assessment revealed Jill's very poor levels of understanding and limited recall even for short simple pieces of information. She struggled with figurative language and with making inferences or understanding consequences. She did not challenge incorrect facts or indicate when she had not understood. Jill's speech was quite unintelligible to strangers and she could only provide a narrative of an event with significant support.

When we arrived at court, the complainant had sent a medical sick note to explain her non-attendance. Jill had been in custody for over 4 months. The judge wanted a relisting within a fortnight, as clearly if Jill was successful in her appeal, she needed to be released at the earliest opportunity. Unfortunately, I was not available for three months. The barrister made an application for bail, and the judge agreed. At least in this way, Jill was not to be punished for delays which were not her responsibility. Her parents and Jill hugged each other and cried when she was released. Three months later I assisted her at the appeal hearing which was successful and she was acquitted.

Dear Court Manager,

I am writing to you following an appeal in your court that was vacated on 31ˢᵗ March as the main complainant was unwell and could not attend. As a matter of urgency, the judge requested a new listing within 2 weeks. I was fully booked for April and May and as a result the hearing was relisted for 27th and 28th June. I apologised for causing this delay.

I am writing to let you know my actual, rather than expected, commitments. In fact, I was available to attend on any date in April.

Week 1 – booked for a trial but the case was vacated and neither the court or the solicitor informed me.

Week 2 – a witness did not arrive for his assessment.

Week 3 – a guilty plea was entered on the preceding Friday, so my witness was not required.

Week 4 – booked for a trial but the case was vacated and I was not informed.

These four cases were in four different areas of England. This was an unusual cluster of cancellations, but not unique and certainly experienced by many other Intermediaries working in the criminal justice system.

Yours sincerely, etc

I wrote this note to the court a couple of years ago. I was perhaps naïve in believing it mattered to the court that my diary was so unpredictable. The judge had clearly been irritated with my lack of availability when he was trying to reschedule. He had requested at the time that I find a replacement. I called the only agency that could possibly respond at such short notice but they had no availability either.

I have seen how complex it is to list hearings and trials when so many players are involved. Getting judges, barristers, police officers and witnesses to fit into a timetable is a tall order. There are also added pressures such as fixed time limits for holding a defendant on remand. Guilty pleas can come at any time, witnesses can be stood down for lots of reasons. I am surprised it works as well as it does!

I have written extensively about the practical complexities for Intermediaries working within the legal system, but I absolutely do not want to give an impression that our profession is alone in struggling. I appreciate, if not as fully as others, that the system often seems to be chaotic, illogical and asking for the impossible. Barristers report working extremely long hours, with impossible deadlines and timescales for digesting thousands of pages of documents. Judges have several hearings to intersperse with a complex trial in progress. CPS barristers are given cases the night before a trial and the recent move to computerised documentation (supposedly limiting the paper) is fraught with complications. This is just a short list of issues, and I am just sharing what I hear and experience second-hand. I have attended a court to be told the judge is not in the building as he has an over-running trial the other side of the city, causing the alleged victim to have to wait another three months for her evidence to be heard. I have arrived at magistrates' court to find that the co-defendant in the case had not been told to attend so the case was postponed. I have assisted a defendant in a five-day trial, where the judge had been allocated to so many hearings or mentions of other cases concurrently during that week, that our trial took an additional three days. I do not have a long-term perspective as I have only worked for six years in the justice system, but am told it is worse than it was. But then this is the experience of most public-sector services in recent years. This is not a party-political point of view, just an observation.

But when it works, it is indeed great. Melanie was an alleged victim of a group of young men who offered drugs to entice her to participate in numerous sexual encounters. She was highly vulnerable in many ways; she had minimal parental support, had not attended school for most of her teenage years and had a history of substance abuse. When I assessed her, she had a very limited understanding of complex language and was easily confused by complex or multi-part questions. Her daily life was chaotic and lacked any routine. I submitted a report to the court with my recommendations and was called to a GRH a fortnight before the trial.

Melanie was a very complex and damaged individual. She was also warned to attend a magistrates' court as a defendant for a breach of her bail conditions in another case and as such, was anxious that the witness appearance did not overlap with this. Being called to two different courts in two different cases as witness and then defendant within one week is a lot to ask of a non-vulnerable person, let alone for someone with Melanie's level of understanding and engagement.

Just as we were waiting to go to court, the court manager reported that he had seen a video of Melanie's aggressive behaviour when she was arrested and suggested that she was too great a risk to be brought into the witness service area before giving evidence. Could she be questioned from another building on a live link, they asked? I explained to the CPS that Melanie had only become aggressive when she had drunk heavily and was being arrested. In this case, she was the alleged victim and certainly not under the influence of any drugs or alcohol. It was vitally important to her not to be seen by the defendants and the best way to do that was in court behind a screen. In a link room, she would be viewed on a large TV monitor in the courtroom and that particular court did not have facilities for any alternative. Melanie, already very stressed by the day's events, said that perhaps she would refuse to give evidence at all.

The court agreed she could enter the building and that witness service would accommodate her despite their concerns. The police officers informed her she was still required, but she again commented, *"I have had enough and may just have to leave the court"* as it was all too stressful.

The court judge for Melanie's case had agreed that all four defence counsel would be required to submit their questions so that I could ensure Melanie would understand them. The first counsel responded the day before the trial with over 130 questions, to which I replied with revisions. The second counsel responded at 9pm the evening before attendance and I replied by midnight. Third counsel sent me questions at 7.30am on the morning of the court attendance.

I met with these three barristers at 10am and it was a very fruitful meeting. We reviewed the revised questions and concluded that cross-examination would last no more than half a day. The fourth counsel did not attend the meeting having decided he would not be asking to cross-examine.

Close to 11am, Melanie was already in the witness service area, very anxious and pacing the floor. I was concerned she might not stay in the building much longer.

Cross examination lasted just two hours. Questions were well put, but I needed to intervene on several occasions as she became more anxious and unable to process even the most basic questions. There were three breaks – Melanie still wanted to get it *'over and done with'* but needed to have a cigarette. By the lunchtime break, she was finished in court. A day of rest before she had her magistrates' court hearing. Interestingly, I had not been requested to assist with this and did not hear from her again.

The court had done its best within the constraints of everyone's busy schedules to accommodate this young woman.

****

At the end of some trials, when there is a guilty verdict, the judge may ask for a pre-sentencing probation assessment and report to assist him in deciding the most appropriate sentence. On some occasions, the judge requests my involvement in this assessment meeting, as he has recognised the value of my input during the trial.

I have mixed feelings about these probation meetings. On the one hand, every probation officer has been delighted to have my assistance in smoothing out the communication issues and the defendant has been more able to respond to the lengthy probation assessment forms. On the other hand, I recognise that I am providing a somewhat artificially enhanced communication environment in which the defendant seems more capable than he would be if unassisted. Nigel, a defendant in a sex abuse case, had been found guilty and I was asked by the judge to attend his pre-sentencing probation assessment. I had spent a lot of time with Nigel as he had been a witness and defendant in separate trials over a period of nine months. I learned a lot from the two-hour session with his probation officer. She was interested in his ability to tell right from wrong, to think about consequences of his actions, what plans and aspirations he had for the future and how he felt about prison. Nigel had lots of incorrect pre-conceived ideas.

When I asked him if he would like me to attend the sentencing hearing, he replied that he would "feel safer". He explained that he knew I would listen for him, check if he understood and he could turn to me if he got stuck.

I had noted that he had improved in his ability to focus over the course of our various court hearings and trials. He was more likely to say when he did not understand, without feeling ashamed or embarrassed. He agreed that now he was more likely to ask, *"What do you mean?"* rather than just bluff it.

****

The practicalities of meeting a defendant who is on remand can be very strange indeed. Oliver had made his first appearance at magistrates' court, and when he was asked his name, the District Judge became concerned about his poor speech and asked for an Intermediary to be appointed. I found out he had been refused bail as the police could not ascertain where he lived. Oliver could not recall his own address. I was told it may be easier to assess him in the court cells, rather than prison. The solicitor reported to me on the appointed morning that Oliver had *'refused to leave his prison cell'*. The next available date was his trial date, so I agreed that I would come along early, carry out an assessment and verbally report my findings to the court.

The venue for assessments vary depending on each case. For vulnerable prosecution witnesses, the assessment usually takes place in a police interview suite, the witness's home, or current residence such as a secure psychiatric unit. If the vulnerable defendant is on bail, the assessment is arranged either in the solicitor's office, whilst a remand defendant will need to be seen in prison. On the few occasions when an assessment must be carried out on the day of the trial, the only available place for an assessment is a court consultation room, usually on the corridor of the court building. Most frustratingly, the court tannoy system sounds into these rooms *'could all parties in the case of Bill and Ben please go to Court One'*, and these announcements can make it very difficult to get a reliable set of observations. For remand defendants like Oliver, the assessment takes place in the court cells meeting rooms.

Getting into the court cells can be a challenge. In many courts, I have been told I cannot visit without the legal representative present, and my professional status is queried. However, when I went to the cells to see Oliver, the security staff were particularly helpful and friendly. In her effort to assist, the security officer took me to one of the larger interview rooms, explaining that Oliver was in a wheelchair. I was not surprised at this, as the referral had mentioned his medical history included 'several Strokes'. The officer on the secure side asked for the name of the prisoner I wanted to see and I gave his full name. Within a few minutes a man arrived, self-propelling his wheelchair. I asked him whether he liked to be called by his first name and he gave me a name I had not heard, so I assumed perhaps this was his middle name or nickname. I asked him, as I ask every client, what he thought this meeting was about. He explained in very clearly articulated speech that he really did not know. He explained about his medications and how he had only been in prison *'since Monday'*. Many of my clients struggle with time concepts, and are very poor narrators of their medication history, so I was not surprised that this did not tally with the referrer's comment that Oliver had been in prison for two months.

We talked for another five minutes before I mentioned his reported history of Stroke. He responded that he had not had a Stroke and proceeded to reveal his amputated leg stump which was the reason for his wheelchair. At this point, it all clicked. I asked his name again and found that his surname was Oliver and this was a case of mistaken identity! The security officer took him back but reprimanded me for using a full name when the prisons only ever used surnames.

I suppose this was another example of miscommunication and assumptions.

When I finally met the real Oliver, it was clear this gentleman was struggling to cope in prison. He had serious cognitive impairments and could not recall the details of his own address, except to mention the area of London. He was extremely thin and spoke about his constant hunger, saying the food in prison was not sufficient for his needs. It is difficult to focus on any intellectual activity when the body is calling out for food. His speech was very limited by the Stroke-induced brain damage, and his concepts of events quite disordered and unreliable.

His solicitor was not particularly receptive to my explanations, but when I joined him and Oliver to discuss the case, I was able to help Oliver to make an informed decision to plead guilty.

Reporting verbally to the court, rather than preparing a written report, is taxing and demands confidence. I personally enjoy the heightened challenge, but it is not for everyone.

When we entered court, the judge took on my recommendations in their entirety and seemed very relieved to have the assistance of an Intermediary. When the sentence was given, taking account of his eight weeks on remand, the judge decided he could be released once probation confirmed his actual address. Oliver told me that his phone, which had been confiscated by the prison, had his sister's number and she would be able to assist.

In Oliver's case, and perhaps others like him, he was on remand because he could not give a permanent address. His brain damage affected this ability, so the police had remanded a very vulnerable man because he was too vulnerable to answer their questions.

****

I was thinking about how my mood is related, sometimes unconsciously, to the way the court has treated these vulnerable people. Although I have said in general I do not spend much energy thinking about the evidence against a defendant, or whether he is likely to be convicted, there are exceptions. I worked with four clients, all defendants, where the facts of the case seemed to take on more significance to me.

I think one of the common threads to these cases, was the seeming waste of public money involved in pursuing cases that either did not seem to have sufficient evidence, or were not, in my humble opinion, in the public interest. I do not have the whole picture of course, and both these matters are for the CPS, not me, to determine.

For each of these four defendants, recovering from the two-year process from arrest to acquittal will take a long time. There were several hearings, many trial days, journeys to solicitors, interviews with police and for one man several months in jail. There were other less obvious impacts too. Joe had not been able to work for 14 months because his security job depended on a clear police record. Finnegan (just 10 years old) had missed many school days, further impairing his poor academic progress. Brendan told me he used to have lots of friends on Facebook, but since the allegations most had blocked him. So much for innocent until proven guilty. Alice's family had moved away as the retribution from neighbours had become too much. These were all people acquitted of the alleged crimes.

****

The police force is dealing with huge increases in non-recent alleged crimes. I am aware of the growing number of elderly people, mostly men, accused of non-recent sexual crimes. I met Cecil, aged 92 years, accused of sexually assaulting his nieces over 45 years ago. I met Cedric, aged 75 years, accused of rape more than 40 years ago. There is little doubt that recent media exposure of celebrity trials has encouraged victims to come forward after many years of emotional angst. I also know that the prisons are not equipped to incarcerate very elderly prisoners and manage their increasing health needs.

When Cecil was due to attend court, my recommendations included several adaptations to the court day. He slept for up to an hour twice a day, had very limited hearing and had poor recall of recent events. As a younger man, both successful in business and highly articulate, he would not have needed an Intermediary. At trial, the court sat for much shorter days, he used a hearing loop and I took notes during the proceedings for him to refer to at the beginning of the subsequent day. When it was time for him to give evidence, he sat down in the witness box, took breaks every 15 minutes and the barristers reviewed their questions in advance with me to keep them relatively simple in structure. I did not envy the judge deciding on sentence when he was convicted by the jury.

Cedric was referred to me by a police officer, who wanted to interview him about allegations from a step-grandchild of events that may have taken place over 30 years ago. Cedric lived in a care home after suffering a Stroke. I assessed him and reported that he was unable to follow simple verbal commands without accompanying gestures, could not challenge an incorrect statement and his 'yes/no' responses were not reliable. The officer reported this back to her inspector who called a halt to further investigations in the case. If true, this must have been a difficult conclusion for the step-grandchild who had finally felt strong enough to report her experience.

"Satisfaction at work depends on levels of control"

I remember a professional development course many years ago, where we were asked to carry out a simple exercise. We were told to draw a large circle on a blank page, which symbolised the whole of our current life. We then drew within the circle the proportion which we felt we had some control over. The facilitator explained that for many people, the level of life satisfaction is directly related to the amount of control they perceive they have over their own activity.

I carried that idea forward in my various roles as manager and company director over the last thirty years. I aimed to increase the levels of control each member of staff had in their work: eg hours of work, booking their leave, or choosing the order they did tasks. It seemed to result in better staff retention and good working relationships.

My experience of working as an Intermediary is that my level of control fluctuates from week to week. I have control over the type and number of cases I accept. The referrals arrive thick and fast but no-one sees my diary or can over-ride my decisions on how much I want to work, or when I take holidays, if I plan several months ahead. So, for example, to get this book finished, I blocked out periods in my diary when I would not take new cases. I can also choose which parts of the country I am prepared to travel to, maybe based on whether I have friends or family nearby. I am mostly able to decide whether I work in the evenings or weekends to write reports, and when I take time off to spend with my grandchildren.

On the other hand, I cannot control whether judges choose to take on my recommendations, or in fact appoint me to assist at court, although I try to set out all the relevant information to inform their decision-making. I cannot predict whether a full week's work will be cancelled at short notice if the defendant pleads guilty or the case is adjourned for other reasons. Consequently, sometimes I find myself without both the expected income or a plan for my week ahead.

When I arrive at the court, like every other person, I am at the mercy of the court timetable. Warned to attend at 9.30am, I may wait until 4pm for a half hour hearing. I may think I am staying in Brighton for a four-day trial and then find myself on my way home by lunch of the first day. I also do not know when each day will finish, and as I choose to take cases across the country, I cannot sign up or commit to any regular evening plans.

The biggest tension is between too many referrals for the number of days in my diary, versus a court that refuses to appoint an Intermediary. In any given February for example, I may hear from two courts that require my attendance on the same week in July, a trial that is going to wait for my next available week in April, or a solicitor who is struggling to explain my lack of immediate availability to a rightly grumpy judge. Meanwhile, another court decides the witness or defendant does not need my services, as a family member can provide the support, or a GRH takes place without my knowledge and the judge refuses many of my recommendations but still insists I attend the trial.

After many years as an employee and middle manager, becoming self-employed was a leap of faith. I had to manage my own diary with vastly competing and ever-changing demands. I had to manage invoicing, chase payments and recognise the variations in cashflow. I invoiced for my first case in early May. I accepted referrals from north, south, east and west, and subsequently collected many train tickets. I stayed in a few hotels but mostly returned home each day. At the end of August, I was still in the red. In other words, a financial cushion is essential. I realise many self-employed jobs involve cash flow management and I have been a company director and charity chair also. I just want to pass on to others starting out or thinking about this work, that without some start-up funds or reserves, it will be a struggle. Those Intermediaries who only work locally have fewer expenses and may have less to worry about, but the vagaries of a government finance department can be very trying. Several years into the work, I still have periods when I am chasing payments for many hours a month. When HMCTS decides to change its systems, such as new codes or new email addresses without letting us know, or police forces introduce new requirements, sometimes several months can go by without any invoices being paid. Intermediaries can be discouraged from accepting work from the 'poor payers'.

The changes in working methods and technology in the 21st Century have made it possible for me to take on cases across England and Wales (and Northern Ireland on occasion).

The mobile smart phone is at the centre of my working life. Without it, I would need to be in my office during office hours, to take calls and answer emails, and to make, change and cancel appointments. I would have to carry a map and plan my route to each court and solicitor's office, and wait until I arrived at a train station to know the best train route, time and platform for departure. Whenever there was a delay or change in plans, my contact with courts, police and solicitors would be dependent on the availability of a public phone box.

Now all these functions are contained in my mobile device, while I am on the move. I can access files, check fares and expenses as part of preparing a quote while away from home, and photograph the expenses receipts for invoicing. I can book, alter and cancel hotels at short notice, check my bank account for payments and respond to queries from finance departments. The matching service at the National Crime Agency send texts when they have a new referral, and it is quick and simple to communicate about cases away from a desk. In fact, I do not really need for a desk or an office at all.

I carry a tablet computer, which is so much lighter and more powerful than its predecessor the laptop. All my files are backed up and I can write my reports while I am away from home. These reports are anonymised during my travel and the client details are only added when I am back connected to a secure network. I am also able to catch up on the intranet for Registered Intermediaries, respond to queries from newly qualified practitioners whom I am mentoring, and read documents for my professional development.

There are other technologies that make it possible to be part of a professional community. Being involved in a regional group is part of continued registration with the MoJ scheme. However, the regions are geographically large and travel is a major impediment to regular participation in meetings. Recently our regional group has started to make use of the available technology, including the introduction of virtual meetings on Google Hangouts and Dropbox for shared documents. This has increased participation and networking for our isolated professional group.

This sense of isolation is similarly reduced by an informal network of colleagues who email and text from across the UK and beyond. I gain a great deal of support, new learning and advice in this way. I mention 'beyond', as I have been providing supervision via emails and Skype to the emerging Intermediary service in New Zealand and this also informs my practice.

Last and by no means least, I pay tribute to the vastly improved public toilets and catering establishments in recent years in the towns and cities of the UK. If I had started this work in the 20th Century, I may have avoided long journeys and been much less flexible in my availability!

"She looks OK to me"

Vulnerability has become a topic of great interest in the non-legal world. Several million people world-wide have viewed Brene Brown's Ted Talk entitled *'On vulnerability'* (11). It is well worth the 20-minute viewing. She speaks eloquently of our human need for connection with others and that these real connections occur when we allow ourselves to show our vulnerability. She argues that our modern society encourages us to hide our vulnerabilities. We strive to feel safe by engaging in cover-ups for our real feelings and emotions, particularly when we are not with our nearest and dearest. I have used these concepts in my work on anger management, as many 'angry' people see vulnerability as a weakness. Vulnerability, as Brene Brown says, is a characteristic our culture encourages us to hide from view. For some of our clients, hiding their vulnerabilities has been a life-long challenge. Most would prefer not to be known as illiterate, simple or crazy. They typically use a variety of techniques and strategies (both passive aggressively and aggressively) to ensure no-one comes too close and spots a weakness.

Identifying their defence mechanisms and avoidance strategies are important points of an Intermediary's assessment, whilst maintaining their dignity in the face of a daunting experience in the criminal system.

In the legal world, the term 'vulnerable' is used quite specifically. The term vulnerable was defined in the Youth Justice and Criminal Evidence Act 1999 (YJCE)(5) on the grounds of age or incapacity.

Physical vulnerability may be obvious. Recognising the connection between communication skills and mental health is less common place. We know that when we are more anxious or stressed, our ability to listen fully and speak fluently is reduced. When we are asked to speak in front of large groups of people, particularly if unaccustomed, we may experience stage fright. When we are anxious about passing a driving test, we know how difficult it is to process all the instructions we are given. In neurological terms, our brain's frontal lobe does not function well under these stressful conditions.

If, however, a person also suffers from Depression, Post-Traumatic Stress Disorder, Personality Disorder, Psychosis, or other mental health conditions, their ability to focus, process and understand language, and then respond effectively, is seriously diminished.

More recently (4) Hon Mr Justice Green commented of the importance of addressing vulnerability. He spoke of the reliance our justice system places on '*the oral tradition*', and so we should '*seek to perfect the process by which a witness gives evidence*'.

I have met barristers who believe they can recognise vulnerability from afar. One told me that the defendant could not possibly be *vulnerable* as he "*had managed to make two babies, hadn't he?*". A judge told me that a defendant could not be vulnerable as *"she was a mother"*. A witness service volunteer, who I had tried to prepare for meeting a very vulnerable young woman recently discharged from a secure psychiatric ward, responded *"she looks OK to me"*.

On being asked to consider the vulnerability of a 25-year old man diagnosed with Post-Traumatic Stress Disorder and Autistic Spectrum Disorder, a Queen's Counsel barrister told me *"I know what vulnerability looks like as I have been involved in many cases with young children. This man is clearly not vulnerable."*

I frequently meet legal professionals who say that once they know the equivalent mental age of a vulnerable witness, they can use their experience of being a parent and work out how to talk to this *"child"*. Being a vulnerable adult does not mean you are a child. Being limited in how you communicate does not make you childlike in your experience of the world.

The YJCE Act specifically refers to the quality of evidence likely to be gained from a potential witness for a case. Achieving this best quality evidence may be very simple. For example, Hilda was an elderly lady who the police officer thought might not be able to give her evidence in court. She had reported to the police that someone known to her had taken funds from her bank account, without her knowledge or consent. The officer requested an Intermediary due to *"her age and possible deterioration in understanding"*. I went with the officer to Hilda's home to complete an assessment of her communication needs. She welcomed me into her living room, which I subsequently discovered was also her bedroom, as she had filled all other spaces with her hoarded possessions. I noticed that Hilda seemed to be lip reading my speech, and when I asked about her hearing, she explained that although she had been offered aids, she preferred not to use them. I sat facing her, raised my voice a little and spoke slowly with emphasised articulation. She responded appropriately, effectively and without any difficulty. She showed me the books she was reading, her crossword puzzles and described her situation coherently. I explained to the police officer that if he were to face her, and speak similarly, the communication would most likely be successful. He was astonished. He was not the only person who has recognised that, with the aid of an experienced communication advisor, vulnerability 'disappears'. Hilda gave her evidence to the police in a written statement. The court decided it did not need her to be cross-examined as there was plenty of other supporting evidence and the defendant pleaded guilty. In this case, an Intermediary was required to assess and advise, but not to be involved any further.

When Joseph was referred to me for assessment he was in the process of gender transition. He had managed his Paranoid Schizophrenia for many years with the help of medication and an excellent care package from social services. His communication was good in the familiar environment of his home. He explained that in the days immediately preceding his fortnightly medication injection (administered by a nurse at the clinic), he was particularly likely to hallucinate, hear voices and lose focus. My advice to the court was simply to plan Joseph's day in court during the first week of his injection cycle to maximise his communication. I did not need to attend court, but the police came back to me reporting that Joseph had '*done really well*' in getting his case across to the jury.

The role of the Intermediary is to minimise the vulnerability, in terms of communication and quality of evidence during the time this person is involved with the court process.

Intermediaries are currently being asked to assess the communication of defendants and witnesses. However, there is a gradual increase in awareness of the vulnerable suspect at the police station. In my work with defendants, I recognise the need for assistance from the earliest point of contact with the legal system. Kevin had been arrested in January when his ex-girlfriend accused him of domestic violence. When he reached the police station, he declined the involvement of a duty solicitor. He was referred to me a few weeks before his trial in a magistrates' court in November. When I met him, I asked him how he had found the interview in the police station. He replied that he had not wanted a solicitor as '*I didn't do anything wrong, so why would I need help?*' Kevin failed many of my tests on verbal reasoning and inference. Clearly, he did not appreciate the value of a lawyer during a suspect interview, whatever the plea.

Like Kevin, Leonard was also charged with assaulting his girlfriend. When his solicitor asked him on the day of trial why he had responded '*no comment*' to all the police interview questions, he replied '*no comment as I didn't want to press charges*'. This may not make sense to you and me, but he believed that she had assaulted him rather than the other way around, and did not appreciate that he might need to explain his actions in court.

These examples show people with an incomplete understanding of the basics of our justice system. It may well be that the general public has a very limited understanding, until they have to engage with it. But when the average communicator needs to know, they have the capacity to ask, read and research. The vulnerable people in this book do not have this resource.

Both Kevin and Leonard were diagnosed with Autistic Spectrum Disorder in their late teens and appreciated having the label. Although they were both well-supported by parents, their schooling and friendships had been a struggle. In court, they were both afforded the assistance of an Intermediary, and both told me that without my explanations of the process of the trial, they would have become angry and aggressive, struggled to stay in the courtroom and certainly would have avoided giving evidence. Kevin managed to hold down a job which had many routine tasks but he struggled with the unpredictability and novelty of the court environment. When the court usher moved in and around the court during the start of his trial, he was very uneasy. He needed a visual list of the order of proceedings and an explanation as the trial progressed.

Malcolm was a competent business and family man until he was seriously injured in a road traffic accident in his mid-twenties. After many months of rehabilitation for brain and limb damage, he functioned well within a family unit where his wife adapted their life to suit his remaining disabilities. He struggled with being in enclosed rooms, speaking with new people and recognising the consequences of his actions. He was advised by rehabilitation professionals that he should always ask for his wife to be present whenever he was in a formal or novel situation. Malcolm spent many hours planning their holidays and researching on the Internet, but liked to have routine in his daily life and withdrew to his bedroom if any unfamiliar people entered the house. Now a man in his forties, he arrived at the assessment session extremely anxious about spending up to an hour in a small meeting room, talking to a new person. He managed to stay for 10 minutes at a time talking directly with me, and then took breaks out in the street while his wife filled in the gaps in his medical history and current needs.

He had been charged with refusing to be breathalysed in a police station. Malcolm was a smart looking and well-dressed man who had been arrested one evening when the police saw him get out of his car and stumble to the curb. When the case reached the court eighteen months later, there was CCTV footage of his refusal to be breathalysed. Malcolm had been encouraged by three officers standing over him, in turn trying to explain his rights and the need for him to agree to the procedure. The language used was complex, jargon-filled and delivered in a routine manner as if reading from a script. Malcolm repeatedly stated that he needed his wife present, as an appropriate adult, and the officers repeatedly stated that an appropriate adult was not necessary for a breathalyser test. Despite his request for an appropriate adult, it was not immediately obvious to the officers that Malcolm was vulnerable.

When a case reaches the solicitors' office, the level of vulnerability can similarly go undetected. On arrest, Norman was not seen by the duty solicitor, but from his police interview where he was allocated an appropriate adult, the solicitor decided to make a referral for an Intermediary assessment. When I met Norman aged 23, he was accompanied by his parents. He had struggled to regularly attend a college course for people with special needs, had not ever been employed and rarely left his house alone. Previous medical records and social service reports showed no conclusive diagnoses, as everyone had found Norman very difficult to assess. From my observations, Norman had little or no understanding of what he was charged with, struggled to give clear responses, or to differentiate whether he did not know or simply did not understand. His lack of ability to understand very simple short pieces of information along with his illiteracy, led to my conclusion that, even with an Intermediary, he would not be able to actively participate in his trial. A subsequent psychiatric report concluded he was unfit to plead. Without the solicitor referral to me, Norman may not have been referred to a psychiatrist.

Olivia was not sufficiently recognised as a highly vulnerable individual. She was an alleged victim in a case of fraud. In her early thirties, she lived alone in a small flat within a social housing block. She had refused all community mental health services despite having a diagnosed psychiatric illness, and spent most of her days caring for her six cats who she described as her *'babies'*. I received a referral after Olivia had given her evidence to the police in an ABE interview. Olivia struggled with paranoid thoughts, had been self-harming for several years and was highly anxious about speaking to any stranger. The male officer involved in the case had not recognised that Olivia struggled to speak with men. Olivia rarely slept at night and was often still sleeping at midday. We developed some rapport during assessment in the police station. Having experienced police arrest many years before, Olivia asked me, *"Why am I here if I haven't done anything wrong?"* Yet another witness who had experience of being a suspect too. We discussed going to visit the court before trial, to acclimatise her and check out the best way for her to cope with cross-examination.

The officer and I planned this court visit for the following week. On the morning, the officer informed me that Olivia had texted that she was not going to go to court, even for a trial. I suggested to the officer that we should visit her at home. He had brought the DVD of her ABE interview to do a 'memory refresh'.

On arrival at her flat, Olivia was initially only prepared to let me in. As an Intermediary, as explained previously, I need to be accompanied by the officer, and so it took some time to persuade Olivia to let us both into her one-room flat. Three hours later I had succeeded in agreeing a plan for her to attend court the following Monday and we had watched the DVD together. The officer had been expecting Olivia to take a taxi to court for an early morning start, but this was not feasible in view of her paranoia and fear of strangers. I was also sure that Olivia would not be able to achieve this early-morning timetable. I suggested that the officer and I would pick her up and I liaised with the CPS office that she would not be expected at court until 1.30pm, a more realistic timing for her cross-examination.

On the morning of the trial I received a call to say the case had been dropped by the CPS. There would be no trial. Olivia was already getting ready to meet us. The unpredictability of the court system again: defendants plead late, witnesses refuse to attend, and reviewing CPS lawyers recognise all too late that there is insufficient evidence. I felt for Olivia; she had put her trust in me, watched the DVD for no purpose and was not likely to feel she had received justice. As previously mentioned, I was not able to visit her, but could only send my best wishes with the officer. Not one of my better days as an Intermediary.

A case study of a defendant

Throughout this book, I have provided brief examples of cases relating to the work of an Intermediary. In this chapter, I want to explore in more detail the full legal process for one defendant, and my involvement.

Susan was 40 years old and had lived with her husband for 22 years. If you had met Susan in a local yoga class, she probably would have presented as a middle-aged housewife with no special needs. She enjoyed the class, kept herself busy at home as a housewife for her husband. In fact, she was more concerned about his welfare, as he was the other defendant with more serious charges in the same trial, than for her own wellbeing. She was charged with 'doing acts tending and intending to pervert the course of public justice'.

The solicitor referred Susan to me and gained prior authority from the Legal Aid Agency to fund my assessment. I met Susan in the solicitor's offices and she was initially very anxious. She told me she had recently changed solicitor and later the solicitor explained that Susan had a significant fear of men, so the firm had now allocated a female solicitor and barrister.

I was presented with two expert reports, both recommending the involvement of an Intermediary. Susan had been declared fit to plead by the psychiatrist and he described her as having 'low mood with suicidal ideation and a full IQ of 72 (12).

I assessed Susan's communication with the solicitor present. She was very focussed on her need for assistance to travel to court and how she would struggle to get up early enough for court. She appeared quiet and anxious on first meeting but gradually became more relaxed and formed a rapport with me. She did not take any medication, except an asthma inhaler which she used infrequently.

My assessment revealed significant auditory processing difficulties, which affected her ability to retain information, make inferences, recognise illogical statements and reach conclusions. She struggled to assert her opinion and was easily swayed when challenged. Her anxiety levels were very high even in the solicitor's office and she reported panic attacks which would likely occur in the court environment.

My report was presented to court and funding was agreed for my attendance at the five-day trial.

I recommended that Susan had the opportunity to see the court, with my assistance, before the trial. This gave visual support and a context to help Susan understand and retain information, by talking about where everyone would sit and what their role would be. As often happens with vulnerable defendants, this was done on the day of the trial, in the ten minutes after the usher opened the courtroom, but before it filled up with barristers and other court personnel.

On the first day of the trial, I met Susan with her parents in the waiting area beside the courtroom. Her husband was accused of pornography related crimes. He sat with her and she was visibly distressed and more focussed on his situation than her own.

The judge permitted a brief GRH at the beginning of the first day. Apart from answering my queries about where I was to sit in the dock (between the two defendants) and where I could stand during evidence, he said that everyone had a copy of my report and could read the recommendations for themselves.

I introduced myself to the prosecution advocate, reiterated that I was employed by the court to assist with communication and that I was not part of the defence team. I suggested that I could advise on his planned questions but he did not take up my offer.

During conferences with Susan's barrister and solicitor, I played an integral part in the process of explaining the quite complex case against her. Susan continued to struggle to maintain focus on her own defence, as she was so anxious for her husband.

When the jury members arrived in court, I sat with her in the dock and reminded her of her right to challenge a juror if she recognised any of them.

Susan's level of anxiety reduced when she could predict what might be happening next. Susan could not remember the plan for a full day, so during the breaks, we identified the expected plan for the next session and I wrote these in a simple list which we ticked off while sitting in the dock.

I provided Susan with blue-tack as a successful stress relief. This is often more acceptable to some judges than a stress 'toy' in the dock. I was also permitted to take my iPad into the dock. This became vital in managing Susan's anxiety and panic attacks, particularly when the prosecution was presenting the pornographic material which formed the major part of the evidence against her husband. As this evidence was not related to charges against Susan and she was so distressed by them, I distracted her with a simple noughts and crosses game. If I had not done this, the court would have needed to adjourn several times while she recovered.

When Susan was distressed, her breathing became laboured and she would whisper to me that she might have to get out of the dock. I encouraged her to use her asthma inhalers and this helped her breathing to settle.

I also filtered out the evidence and parts of the trial that did not relate directly to her. I would say, *"this bit isn't very important, I will take notes and tell you in the break"*.

Without this filtering, Susan would have been more distressed and would have lost focus on the particularly relevant parts of the evidence against her. The whole trial could not realistically be slowed to her pace, nor would it have been practical for language be simplified throughout.

[My behaviour in the dock is interpreted by some judges in one of two ways: if I whisper only some of the time, some judges observe that I am not *'translating everything'* – which of course would be like being an interpreter and not useful to defendants like Susan, who need some filtering to avoid being overloaded as they cannot process large amounts of information. On other occasions when I do not speak in the dock at all, perhaps because the defendant and I have agreed that I would make notes and talk it through in the breaks, some judge conclude that I do not seem to be *'doing anything'*. In Susan's case, I needed to define the key points and all that was relevant for her.]

In conference, her barrister spent a couple of meetings ensuring she understood the sentencing possibilities which had been discussed with the prosecutor and her options in terms of plea. I helped to simplify this sufficiently for Susan to make an informed decision.

When in the dock, if Susan commented on the proceedings, I wrote notes and then assisted her in telling the barrister in conference during a break. She would not have been able to either remember or make written notes herself. On several occasions, she made observations that significantly affected the way the defence team presented her case.

When evidence such as written statements, transcripts, maps, diagrams and pictures were presented to the jury and the court, I had to indicate to the usher that I needed a copy to share with the defendant. Because there had not been a full GRH, this direction had not been given by the judge. I made a note on these documents of any comments that Susan made and assisted her to relate this to her legal team. With shorter documents, I assisted her to find the place on written material and highlight the important parts. With longer documents, we discussed them wherever there was time in a break.

Sitting beside Susan, it was easy for me to monitor her emotional state and draw the judge's attention to any difficulties she was having or if she needed a break. I raised my hand until the judge noticed. The judge had agreed at the GRH that Susan would be permitted to leave promptly but, on two occasions, he continued for another ten minutes before allowing an adjournment, by which time Susan was having a panic attack.

On day four, Susan was due to go into the witness box. We had 10 minutes in the empty court during an adjournment to practise neutral questions. I stood beside the witness box throughout her questioning.

My recommendations for this part of the trial included:

- Use simple, everyday words and phrases;
- Keep to a clear chronology;
- Introduce each topic and give Susan time to refocus;
- Ask your questions at a slow pace, as Susan needs time to process each part;
- Pause between questions;
- Allow time for Susan to process the question and formulate the answer. Repeating the question too soon will be detrimental to her processing of the question;
- Keep sentences short, with 3 key words maximum;

- Avoid complex sentence types we know she has difficulty understanding;
- Avoid front-loaded questions and preambles that make questions unnecessarily long;
- Avoid tag questions e.g. "it's raining, isn't it?" or "it isn't snowing, is it?";
- Avoid negatives, phrase questions positively whenever possible;
- Avoid non–literal language;
- Avoid acronyms and abbreviations;
- In order to check that Susan has understood, ask her to explain.

During examination in chief, I did not need to intervene as the defence barrister had taken on the model of communication I had used during our many conferences and adapted her language very successfully. During cross-examination by the prosecution barrister, I intervened on several occasions, and rephrased questions when the judge permitted.

After 30 minutes, I asked for a break at a convenient point in the questioning, as I considered that Susan was losing focus and her anxiety was rising dramatically. The judge accepted this, but once the jury had left the court, he told the advocates that his case management had been interfered with by the Intermediary and he would not now be able to complete closing speeches that day as he had planned. He did not address me directly but spoke as if I were not in the room. However, Susan took a break and returned more composed and able to understand the questions.

The jury reached a verdict within a couple of hours. Susan and her husband were found guilty. Her husband was sentenced and led away to custody immediately. The judge accepted the request from Susan's barrister that a pre-sentencing probation assessment would assist the judge with her sentence. Funding was found for me to assist at the probation meeting several weeks later. The probation officer mentioned how useful she had found the assistance of a communication adviser, and in her report, she suggested that Susan be introduced to the local adult learning disability team as part of a package of plans for her conditional discharge. The judge agreed.

Although this was a life-changing and traumatic event for Susan, and as usual I did not have an opinion about the verdict, I consider she was only able to participate effectively and receive a fair trial with the assistance of an Intermediary.

"They just don't get it!"

So, who doesn't get it?

- The barrister who thinks a mentally ill person should be consistent in the presentation of his vulnerability;

- The vulnerable witness who has very limited understanding of the process for giving evidence and being cross-examined;

- The solicitor who thinks that being able to speak means being able to understand;

- The vulnerable suspect who does not request a legal representative as he '*hasn't done anything wrong*',

- The vulnerable defendant who pleads guilty as he doesn't think he can sit in the dock for four days;

- The police officer who fails to recognise that managing in a comfortable interview suite talking to one person is not the same as being cross-examined via a live link;

- The judge who thinks she can analyse grammar and vocabulary whilst carrying out other vital aspects of her role simultaneously;

- The judge who thinks a family relative and an experienced barrister can be sufficiently skilled to ensure effective participation of a defendant who cannot retain more than 50% of the evidence he hears, let alone manage the simplest verbal reasoning tasks;

- The witness service volunteer with limited experience of mental health issues, who has not been sufficiently trained or appropriately allocated;
- The Intermediary when she sees herself as part of the defence team;
- The Intermediary who assesses her own effectiveness in terms of the conviction of a perpetrator, or when she recoils from assisting an alleged rapist or murderer.

Potentially everyone doesn't get it. There is clearly an increasing number who do, and I hope this trend will continue.

One of my standard questions toward the end of an assessment meeting with a witness or defendant is *'How are you feeling about going to court?'* Jacob replied, *"I can do this if you help me understand"*. Jacob had managed to get through school, just under the radar like many of the vulnerable defendants I have worked with. Aged 25, he had never had a job and was currently living alone in a small flat. He described his 'routine' as spending most of the night on his computer and most of the day sleeping. He rarely ate a meal, mostly snacking on crisps and cake, and rarely walked further than the local shop when he needed cigarettes. He had lost contact with his family and although known to community mental health services, he had no regular support.

Jacob was accused of harassment after he approached the receptionist at the homeless hostel, where he had previously lived. The trial was listed for one day the following month. He had not been arrested before, and he told me that he was petrified of court and being asked to speak up in front of so many people.

Although he had seen his solicitor a couple of times, he was very poorly informed or had failed to retain the information. He had refused a legal representative at the police station, as he '*hadn't done anything wrong*', and no one had suggested an appropriate adult.

Jacob's assessment revealed poor auditory processing of new information; for example, when I told him a short story about a mother and her two children in less than 100 words using simple vocabulary, he struggled to recall any specific information immediately afterward. This was in a quite relaxed environment of a solicitor's office, with just one person listening. He struggled to provide any narrative of his daily activity and had a poor concept of time. These were not surprising as he was probably seriously sleep deprived, malnourished and lacked any structure to his day.

Jacob was clear he needed help at court and wanted information. The leaflet sent from the court was too complex for his limited literacy. I drew a simple line drawing of the magistrates' courtroom, labelled the people and then described the trial as a football match with two halves. He took up the offer of keeping this diagram when we finished the meeting.

At court, I arranged for us to go into the empty courtroom before the morning session started. We looked around and checked out who would be sitting in each place. He tried out being in the witness box, practiced the oath and answered some basic neutral questions. He tried out the seat and decided he would prefer to stand when he gave evidence.

I reminded him that during the first half of the trial, we would be listening and he would not be required to speak. This is a basic misunderstanding of many clients – they imagine that the entire trial will be cross-examination. We met with his counsel and I helped him understand the choices he was being offered regarding his plea. Counsel was not keen for Jacob to give evidence, unsure how he would come across to the magistrates. One of the significant advantages of Intermediary involvement, I believe, is that defendants are more likely to give evidence with assistance of the Intermediary, who will ensure he understands the questions and that the court recognises his vulnerability.

Jacob had his chance to address the magistrates, and he explained how he had not intended to harass the hostel receptionist, but had been wanting a quick chat as he was feeling lonely.

Information is power. Vulnerability, almost by definition, means lack of power. Information delivered in the usual ways eg leaflets, letters and long explanations do not work for a functionally illiterate and very limited communicator, and of course being told to *"say if you don't understand"* or *"ask me about anything you want to know"* does not work when you do not know you have misunderstood or cannot hold on to an explanation long enough to make sense of it.

****

So, what does the future hold? Any underlying belief that Intermediaries are an expensive luxury for all but the 'extremely rare' cases misses the point. Access to justice is a human right, and effective participation does not mean simply being physically present in the dock for a day (or several weeks) waiting for a verdict.

Training for legal professionals – barristers, solicitors, and judges – will certainly improve matters. There is a danger that this training results in a 'one model fits all' approach. The Advocates Gateway (13) has excellent Toolkits providing generalised advice on good practice with vulnerable people, but in many courts, I hear *'well we have all read the Toolkit...'* intimating that an Intermediary will not be required once a clinical definition or label been matched with the appropriate toolkit. For example, if Chloe is diagnosed as Autistic, follow the Toolkit on Autism. But Chloe also has a hearing loss and Post-Traumatic Stress Disorder, so which toolkit does the court follow? John does not have a diagnosis, as he passed under the radar at school. In many cases, the toolkits are not an alternative to a specialised Intermediary, but certainly a good starting point when no intermediary is available.

The current system of self-employed Registered Intermediaries, trained by the MoJ has many limitations. Of course, as has been described in previous chapters, the scheme currently only serves witnesses in criminal cases. In the six years that I have been working in this field, we have been expecting an imminent equitable service for defendants, but I do not see anything coming soon.

Self-employed professionals with no supervision, management structure, quality control or on-going centralised training does not bode well for the development of the service. The current system has two methods of evaluating and maintaining standards: a satisfaction survey sent to the police and CPS, though not to advocates or the judiciary, and a continued professional development log submitted annually. Both methods are useful if they are part of a more comprehensive system, but if we asked a nurse to comment on the professional competence of a physiotherapist, we would not call that maintaining quality standards. The profession needs peer review and observations as well as feedback from the real users of the service – the vulnerable people and their families.

As a matter of course, I now ask the vulnerable defendant or witness to tell me whether, and if so how, my presence has made any difference to their experience of the justice system. Of course, in some cases, it is more appropriate to ask their families and carers. I ask them before there is a verdict, as that might affect their opinion. A very small minority tell me they would have managed without my assistance. Most make it clear that I have helped them increase their sense of dignity, understanding and massively reduced their fear, allowing them to participate as best they could. They often say it has been *"fairer"*.

Roaming around the country, self-employed and working in isolation is also not a long term option. It has suited me in the latter part of my working life. Not every Intermediary roams, or likes train travel as much as I do. But I doubt the unpredictability suits many people and certainly not as a long-term career. Retention of Registered Intermediaries is poor with many leaving soon after recruitment and many who take on this role do so on a part-time basis or are near to retirement.

A professional representative body for all Intermediaries – Intermediaries for Justice (IfJ) (15) – is certainly a way forward and will hopefully develop significantly in the next few years. IfJ is the only national provider of conferences for Intermediaries since the MoJ stopped its involvement in this part of Continuous Professional Development of Registered Intermediaries. Their website is a good source of information about how to access an Intermediary and many aspects of our work.

Those lawyers who are less resistant to change are radically altering their communication style. There are campaigns to remove the glassed docks for all but the high-risk defendants; pre-recording of cross-examination ahead of trial (section 28) will alleviate some issues and, I believe create some new ones. The Ministry of Justice has a court reform programme over the next 5-6 years which includes modernising the court system. The legal system, steeped in ritual and tradition, does change, just very slowly.

George's gave his evidence in a crown court. The defence barrister adapted her questions to my recommendations. The prosecutor had resisted my attempts to advise him on question structure and vocabulary beforehand, and asked George, *"Do you think this injury is consistent with a bang on the head?"* I intervened, asking for the word '*consistent*' to be simplified. The prosecutor said, '*George, you know what consistent means, don't you?*' The judge did not intervene. I felt I could not do more without the judge's support. George replied '*Yes*'. His defence barrister asked one re-examination question: '*What does 'consistent' mean?*' George replied, '*I have no idea!*' With the help of an astute barrister who had spent time with George's intermediary, the jury heard George's best evidence. We cannot depend on a poor communicator to alert the court when language is too complex.

I have focussed on the criminal jurisdiction for most of this book. Meanwhile family court requests for Intermediaries are rapidly increasing, and civil courts and tribunals are just catching on. We have come a long way in the beginning of the 21st century but there is plenty more to do. Being part of a group of people contributing to a more just system for vulnerable people has been, and will continue to be, a privilege.

What now?

Now have your say.

www.facebook.com/theyjustdontgetit;

Email to **theyjustdontgetit.paulabacken@gmail.com**;

Twitter at TjdgiPaula.

Perhaps I haven't said enough about assisting police to interview vulnerable witnesses, maybe you have been bothered by lack of information about working with children in the justice system, or maybe you have experience of working with an Intermediary. I hope there will be contributions from clients of Intermediaries or those who have struggled with attending court without an Intermediary.

I look forward to hearing from you and thanks for reading this far.

Notes

1. Intermediaries in the Criminal Justice System – improving communication for vulnerable witnesses and defendants by Joyce Plotnikoff and Richard Woolfson, pub Policy Press 2015. Or visit www.lexiconlimited.co.uk.

2. See www.justice.org.uk/in-the-dock – reassessing use of dock in criminal trials.

3. This was a circulated but unpublished document, "Number Crunching", based on over 450 defendant cases, when I was employed by Communicourt Ltd (2011-2015). It details other statistics on this population.

4. Addressing Vulnerability in Justice Systems, Ed by P Cooper and L Hunting pub by Wildy, Simmonds and Hill 2016.

5. Youth Justice and Criminal Evidence Act 1999 at https://www.eradar.eu/youth-justice-and-criminal-evidence-act-1999

6. In a survey conducted by the National Crime Agency matching service with referring officers in 2016, the Intermediary services were described as 'excellent' by 88% of respondents and 'more than satisfactory' by an additional 11%.

7. HMCTS is Her Majesty's Court and Tribunal Service and is a central funding route for court-related defendant work.

8. I have a long-standing working relationship as a former deputy director with Communicourt Ltd. I am not able to access similar information for Triangle (www.triangle.org.uk), which specialises in children and young people up to 25 years of age.

9. 'Three Girls' on BBC in May 2017.

10. J Gregory & K Bryan 'Speech and Language Therapy intervention with a group of persistent and prolific young offenders in a non-custodial setting with previously undiagnosed

speech and language and communication difficulties. 2011 International Journal of Language and Communication Disorders Vol 46 (2) 202-15)

11. View www.ted.com/talks/brene_brown_on_vulnerability.

12. Full IQ is often measured with a range of sub tests in assessments such as the Wechsler Adult Intelligence Scale (WAIS).

13. Visit www.theadvocatesgateway.org for more information on the use of Intermediaries across the justice system.

14. 'Directions to appoint an Intermediary for a defendant's evidence will thus be rare, but for the entire trial extremely rare.' (3F.13; [2016] England and Wales Court of Appeal CRIM 97).

15. Visit www.Intermediaries-for-justice.org for more information about the Intermediary in the Justice System.

Glossary

1. In Crown and Magistrates' court:

<u>Witness</u> = *a person who has some evidence to tell the court. This could be the alleged victim or someone else who was present or has knowledge that will help others to know about the case.*

<u>Defendant</u> = *a person who has been accused of committing a crime.*

<u>Co-defendant</u> = *other persons who have been accused and are being tried in the same case.*

<u>Crown Prosecution Service</u> (CPS) = *this body decides if a case proceeds to trial, and then provides a lawyer to act as prosecutor. This is not the victim's representative as is commonly believed, but the lawyer who acts on behalf of the state to bring all the evidence against the defendant.*

<u>Counsel / advocate</u> = *a barrister, solicitor advocate or solicitor depending on trial.*

<u>Defence counsel</u> = *the lawyer who represent the defendant.*

<u>Conference</u> = *this meeting between defendant and lawyer may occur before the trial and during any break in the trial proceedings.*

<u>Jury</u> = *a group of twelve randomly selected people who are given the task of deciding whether the defendant(s) is guilty or not guilty.*

<u>Verdict</u> = *guilty or not guilty.*

<u>Sentence</u> = punishment decided by the judge / magistrates.

<u>Evidence</u> = *any information that assists the court in understanding the case. This could be in written form, pre-recorded, or from a witness who answers questions in court.*

<u>Evidence-in-chief</u> = *the evidence that is given by each witness from their recollection and point of view. The counsel for the CPS will ask questions of a prosecution witness or victim, while the defence counsel will ask questions of the defendant or defence witness.*

<u>Cross-examination</u> = *after evidence-in-chief, this is when counsel from 'the other side' challenges the evidence given by the witness. So, prosecution witnesses or alleged victims will be cross-examined by defence counsel, and defence witnesses or defendants will be cross-examined by CPS counsel.*

<u>Dock</u> = *the area where the defendant usually sits throughout the trial. Often locked and surrounded by glass. The defendant is expected to be in the dock for all hearings and all parts of the trial.*

<u>Witness box</u> = *the area where each witness sits or stands and gives evidence. When the defendant is to be questioned, he goes to the witness stand as he is a witness in his case.*

<u>Court usher</u> = *a member of court staff who assists in the smooth running of the court eg bringing witnesses and juries into the courtroom, distributing documents and assisting with administering the oath.*

<u>Security dock officer</u> = *a uniformed guard who will bring the defendant from the cells if he is in custody, and keep guard of all defendants throughout the trial. Depending on risk, and numbers of defendants, there may be more than one dock officer.*

<u>Officer-In-the-Case</u> (OiC) = *the police officer who has taken the lead in the case, and is often called to the witness stand as a prosecution witness. He / she may be present for much of the trial, assisting the CPS barrister with paperwork and additional evidence.*

<u>Interviewing officer</u> = *the police officer who took the evidence from either a witness or a defendant. There may be more than one for each case.*

<u>Achieving Best Evidence</u> (ABE) = *the recorded interview of a witness or alleged victim. This is an alternative to a written statement in most situations, and is frequently used for vulnerable witnesses.*

<u>Solicitor</u> = *the legal representative of the defendant from the beginning of the case through to trial and beyond.*

2. Differences between Magistrates and Crown Courts:

There are many differences between magistrates and crown courts, so I have just described the basics to help the reader who has limited knowledge of the court system.

- There is no jury in a magistrates' court; the verdict is decided by the district judge or magistrates.

- There may be a district judge or three (occasionally two) magistrates who sit in judgement of and reach a verdict; in a crown court, there is one judge.

- A legal advisor in a magistrates' court, advises on the law and administration. In the crown court, a court clerk assists with administration.

- The magistrates' courtroom is less formal; for example, there are only wigs and gowns in crown court.

- All cases start in the magistrates' court. The case may move to crown court for various reasons, often the seriousness of the charges.

Printed in Great Britain
by Amazon